ReCraft

How to turn second-hand stuff into beautiful things for your home, family and friends

Frances Lincoln Ltd
www.franceslincoln.com

ReCraft
Copyright © Frances Lincoln Limited 2012
Text copyright © Sara Duchars and Sarah Marks 2012
Illustrations copyright © Nicola Kent 2012
Photographs copyright © Dan Duchars 2012
with additional photography by Maxwell Attenborough
First Frances Lincoln edition 2012

British Library Cataloguing-in-Publication data
A catalogue record for this book is available from the British Library.

ISBN: 978-0-7112-3356-0

Printed and bound in China

9 8 7 6 5 4 3

MIX
Paper from
responsible sources
FSC® C008047
FSC
www.fsc.org

ReCraft

How to turn second-hand stuff
into beautiful things
for your home,
family and
friends

buttonbag

SARA DUCHARS
SARAH MARKS

illustrations by
Nicola Kent

FRANCES LINCOLN LIMITED
PUBLISHERS

Buttonbag

Sara Duchars and Sarah Marks, the founders of Buttonbag, started sewing when they were children and never really stopped. Even when they were living in Spain – they met in a bar in Barcelona twenty years ago – they had their trusty Singer sewing machines with them and collaborated on various projects. They started Buttonbag when they returned to the UK, making and selling craft kits.

In the six years since selling its first ever craft kit at London's Greenwich market, Buttonbag has grown to become one of the country's leading craft companies. Buttonbag designs and manufactures a wide range of craft kits aimed at children and adults and has over five hundred stockists in the UK.

"In the early days, we used to cut all the fabric by hand on the kitchen table and by Friday evening every surface in both our houses would be covered with scraps of material, wool and sequins as we got ready for the weekend craft market. As we got bigger we started looking for premises and moved into a studio near London Fields in Hackney – not far from the heart of the old textile manufacturing district in the East End. In fact some of our favourite suppliers are just round the corner."

Buttonbag HQ (Left to right): Maddy, Sara, Sarah, Jody, Paula, Anna, Naomi

"I've always loved making things. Many of my earliest memories are of things I made; a viking village populated by peg dolls, glove puppets, a zoo out of lolly sticks and plasticine, doll's house furniture from matchboxes, a canoe for my Action Man.... My parents taught me a lot of stuff. My mum showed me how to knit and my dad, who had trained as a tailor, taught me how to sew when I was about six. I remember him showing me how to cut a pattern for perfectly-fitting trousers for my Action Woman. He was also pretty good at dressing-up costumes (left). I think both me (Punch and Judy show) and my sister (the crocodile) might have won prizes for these ones. I still love making stuff. In fact I get a bit nervous if I'm not in the middle of a making project."

Sarah

"When I was little my mum used to make all my dresses, and she would also make a matching dress for my doll. She always had a project on the go, and, consequently, so did I, be it sewing, knitting, crocheting or embroidery. My main love was sewing, and encouraged by my mum, I started making my own clothes as a teenager and this led me to train as a tailor, and then to work in the costume department of the Royal Opera House. I still always like to have a current project, and encourage my children to do the same. As well as the actual enjoyment of making things, I still get the same sense of achievement now as I did when I was a child."

Sara

This book

ReCraft, the book, arose from a project Buttonbag undertook to design a range of craft kits for the charity Oxfam. We visited our local branch and bought armfuls of all the things you can find in just about any second-hand shop: cardigans, men's stripey shirts, old records, plastic bangles, denim jackets, floral curtains, tweed skirts, a lonely cup and saucer. We took them back to Buttonbag HQ and set about turning our finds into beautiful things for our friends, families and homes. Jumpers became tea cosies, shirts were turned into metres and metres of beautiful bunting, old records were melted into funky bowls, a penguin hatched from a woolly black jumper, the cardigan was transformed into baby bootees and a matching hat and mittens. It was a hugely rewarding and creative process and resulted in a range of ReCraft kits now available through Oxfam. We also realized we had more than enough ideas for a book. *ReCraft* is that book.

Why ReCraft?

The increasing popularity of craft during the last decade seemed to take a lot of people by surprise, but we're pretty sure that the new-found love for all things handmade is not a fad. At Buttonbag we think craft is a vital antidote to today's fast-paced life whose rhythms are dictated by consumerism and technology. We are not anti-tech – our children play computer games, our husbands covet all the latest gadgets and we spend a good part of every day on the computer, phone and internet. But sewing, knitting and making stuff help balance it all out.

Craft means a lot of different things to different people but to us it's about making things. It's about the process of making them as well as the end result, creating as well as the creation. In fact, quite often we don't know exactly what we are making until we've made it. (And sometimes we don't like what we've made.) It's about experimenting with fabric, sewing, glue, paper and wool.

ReCraft takes this one step further. It's about using your hands and imagination to give old things a new lease of life. It's a way of recycling things you might otherwise throw away – or things other people have given away. Over the next pages we want to show you how even the most uninspiring objects can be transformed by the work of your own hands; holey jumpers, old shirts, dusty books, chipped cups, battered spoons, floral curtains, scratched records and broken games can become soft toys, candles, secret boxes, precious jewels, cushions and bags.

The concept of ReCrafting has been with us for a long time – often driven by necessity. Think about the years of rationing when thrifty sewers ran-up a New Look-inspired frock from a pair of curtains or parachute silk was hoarded for wedding dresses. But ReCraft is also a very modern, even rebellious way of being creative. ReCrafted projects will always be unique because they will inevitably be steeped in the character of the original material. Even if you follow the instructions for a project in this book, it will probably turn out differently from ours because you are starting with something you found.

We love the way ReCraft means asking, "What can I turn this into?" rather than, "What do I need to make this?" Take, for example, the soft toy projects at the beginning of the book. We didn't set out to make cats, pigs, whales, penguins and frogs. It was the colour and texture of the jumpers that triggered those designs. You may discover your second-hand finds will inspire all kinds of ideas of your own. Your jumpers might shout bunny, zebra and platypus. We hope you enjoy making them.

What you can do

Great craft ideas rarely start in the haberdashery department – although you will certainly need to visit them for essentials. Instead see your local charity shop or jumble sale as the source of all kinds of raw craft materials. Don't worry if they look uninspiring on the rail or in the sales basket – it's your skills and imagination that will transform them. You don't need a cashmere jumper – a plain acrylic one will do. And you can wash it! Similarly the bunting and cushions were made from completely average men's shirts – striped, checked and plain. It's amazing how much you can make from just one large shirt!

However, if you do see anything in a Liberty print, or a lovely floral fabric grab it. Some of the projects, such as the wrapped bangles, covered notebooks and pin-cushions, only need a tiny amount of fabric so it's worth making them in something beautiful.

Use what you can find and remember that wild colours and wacky pattern combinations can add a totally different feel to a project. A penguin doesn't have to be black and white! The beauty of ReCrafting is that you're not investing in expensive materials, so don't be afraid to experiment. Mix and match elements from different projects – a bird from the baby bird mobile can also be a Christmas decoration, the heart template can be cut twice, sewn together and stuffed to create a lovely pin-cushion.

Some of the projects draw on traditional skills like sewing and knitting, such as the t-shirt rug and the aprons, but there are plenty that don't involve any needle and thread at all. We love the record bowls and the Lego clock, the spoon and fork hooks and the toy box jewellery.

If you are making something for a baby or toddler think about how it will be used. Ensure that all small parts are extremely well sewn on and cannot be pulled off and swallowed. Embroider eyes on soft toys rather than sewing on buttons and make sure that no stuffing will escape. Using washable material or wool is a good idea too.

A second-hand shirt
is the ReCrafter's
best friend.
Striped, spotted,
checked or plain,
a cotton shirt can
be turned into all
kinds of things . . .

Baby bird
mobile
p.32

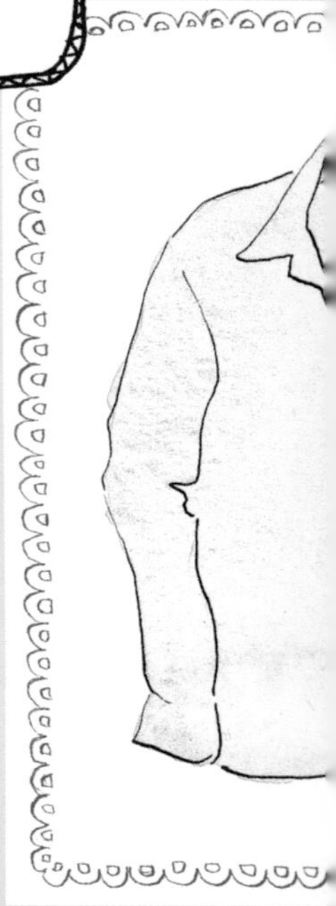

Shirt
cushions
p.58

Aprons
pp.46-9

Bunting
p.60

Cotton reel
pin-cushions
p.100

... like bunting, cushions,
children's mobiles, aprons,
pictures and pin-cushions and
more.

Button
picture
p.94

Basic sewing kit

If you are an experienced sewer you will already have your favourite sewing stuff close to hand, however if you are just getting started it can sometimes seem like you need an awful lot of equipment. You don't. These are the basic tools that you will use again and again in all our sewing projects and they are all easy to find and inexpensive. Having said that, the one item it is worth spending money on is a good pair of scissors. There is nothing more frustrating than blunt scissors and accurate cutting is vital in order to achieve a straight hem!

Scissors – it is best to have two pairs, a small pair for snipping thread and a larger pair for cutting fabric. Try not to use your fabric scissors for cutting anything else like paper or card as this will only blunt them.

Needles – a mixed pack, usually called household needles, is perfect. It will have different lengths and thicknesses. You will need bigger needles with big eyes for some projects, and thin sharp needles for other projects.

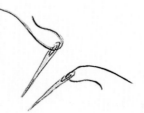

Thimble – some people prefer not to use a thimble but others can't manage without it. If you can get used to using a thimble it will make sewing easier on your fingers.

Pins – we find longer pins with round coloured heads, often called glass headed, are the easiest to use. Safety pins are useful too.

Pencils – dressmaker's pencils or tailor's chalk are very useful for marking on fabric, and you will need ordinary pencils too.

Sewing thread – we use both sewing thread and embroidery thread in our projects. Buy as you need and you will soon build up a collection of different colours. Embroidery thread can also be split to make it thinner.

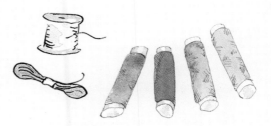

Tape measure – either a retractable one or a long tape. A ruler is also useful for drawing straight lines.

Sewing machine – don't be tempted to buy one that can do lots of fancy stitches. You will never use them. Buy the best machine you can afford that does straight stitch and zig-zag. You will probably never bother with button-holes either, once you realise that most clothes can avoid them with the use of hook-and-eye clasps, zips and Velcro.

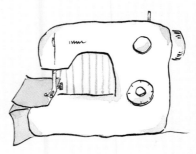

Basic stitches

Running stitch – this is probably the stitch which is most useful for the hand sewer. For a strong seam make the stitches small and close together. For a temporary stitch to hold fabric in position before you finish it for good – known as tacking or basting – make the stitches longer so they can be easily pulled out. Thread the needle with about 40cm/16in of thread and tie a knot at one end. Push the needle from the underside of the fabric to the top. Gently pull the thread tight – the knot will stop it going all the way through. Push the needle back through from the top to the bottom about 5mm/¼in along. Make the second stitch in the same way about 5mm/¼in along again. To finish make a few stitches on the spot to stop the thread from unravelling.

Gathering stitch – this is a running stitch, using longer stitches, which are then pulled tight to gather the fabric up. The bigger the stitches, the bigger the gathers.

16

Over and over stitch – as the name suggests, this stitch is done by sewing over and over the edge of one or two pieces of fabric. It is also a good stitch for sewing on patches. Thread the needle with about 40cm/16in of thread and tie a knot in the end. Push the needle from the underside of the fabric to the top. Pull the thread tight and take it over the edge of the fabric and push the needle back in from the underside of the fabric about 5mm/¼in along. To finish, make a few small stitches on the spot to stop the thread unravelling.

Blanket stitch – this is a traditional stitch used for the edging on woollen blankets. It is very useful for making a decorative edge and for holding two pieces of felt or wool together. Push the needle in about 5mm/¼in away from the edge of the fabric and, holding the thread along the edge of the fabric, bring it out again, making sure the thread is behind the needle. Pull tight and repeat.

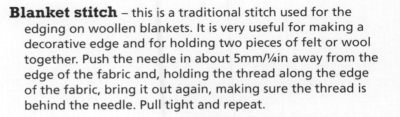

Back stitch – this is a useful stitch when you want to make a seam very strong. We also use it for hand sewing soft toys and other things made out of jumpers. Make a running stitch, then bring the needle up again, the same distance away from the end of the stitch. Now do a back stitch – take the needle back down at the end of the first stitch. Repeat.

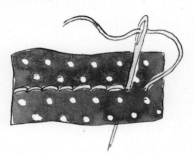

Basic techniques

Sewing a seam – lay the two pieces of fabric together, and machine or hand sew a running stitch about 1.5cm/½in from the edge. Do some stitches on the spot at either end to stop the stitches unravelling. Press the seam open with an iron after sewing.

Sewing a hem – if the fabric frays, it is best to turn it up twice – this is easiest if you press it with an iron, first 1.5cm/½in then another 1.5cm/½in. Then machine or hand sew a running stitch all the way along.

Notching – these are small triangular cuts made in the hem or seam that make the fabric lie more smoothly. These are particularly useful on curved seams. Snip little triangles out before turning the fabric the right way. Be careful not to snip through any stitches.

Threading ribbon through a channel – make sure the channel you have sewn is wide enough to take the ribbon or elastic you want to use. Attach a safety pin to one end, then push it into the channel, and gradually push it all the way round, pulling the ribbon behind it. Make sure you don't let the other end of the ribbon disappear in the channel.

Making a pleat – a pleat is often useful to make something look fuller, or more three-dimensional. It is basically a fold in the fabric. You can fold the fabric over to the side, then stitch down, or fold two sides in to the middle before sewing across the top to hold in place.

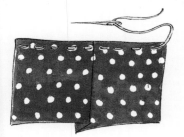

Appliqué – this is a very useful technique for decorating clothes, blankets, the tea cosies – basically anything which you want to prettify with some scraps of fabric, or to cover up a hole in your favourite pair of jeans. The best fabrics to use are those which don't fray, such as felt or t-shirt fabric. Other fabrics can either be turned in at the edges, or left with a raw edge. Use the templates or create your own designs. To make the fabric stiffer iron on some interfacing, which also prevents fraying. If you use Bondaweb (or similar iron-on transfer adhesive product) you can stick the patch where you want it simply by ironing it on. Otherwise dab on a bit of fabric glue, or just pin and sew. Use an over and over stitch, or a running stitch.

Stuffing – you can buy toy stuffing from any good haberdashers, or you can use bits of old socks or fabric scraps, but these must be cut up *very* small so the soft toy doesn't bulge out in odd places. Leave a small opening when sewing, and push the stuffing in through the hole. You might want to use a blunt pencil or a knitting needle to push the stuffing right up in to the corners. When the item looks fat enough, sew the hole closed.

Projects

Each project has been given one, two or three buttons, indicating the level of skill required

- Simple and easy – only basic skills needed
- Moderate – some simple machine sewing may be necessary
- Advanced – more complicated techniques involved

TOYS

24   **Whale**
25   **Cuddly penguin**
26   **Frog**
28   **Pig**
29   **Kitten**

BABY STUFF

32   **Baby bird mobile**
34   **Baby hat, mittens and booties**
36   **Baby bag and play mat**
40   **Patchwork baby blanket**
42   **Dodos**

FAMILY

46   **Frilly pinny**
48   **Cook's apron**
48   **Children's chef's hat**
49   **Children's aprons**
50   **Scrabble magnets**
51   **Lego clock**
52   **Tea and egg cosies**
54   **No-sew balaclava**
56   **Hoodlets**
58   **Shirt cushions**
60   **Bunting**
62   **Deckchairs**
64   **Beach bag**
66   **Jam jar candles**
67   **Glitter cup candles**

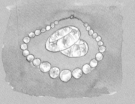

FRIENDS

70	**Old book handbag**
72	**Tweedy satchel**
74	**Kelly bag**
75	**Fabric flower corsage**
76	**Toy box jewellery**
80	**Granny purse**
81	**Envelope purses and bags**
82	**Silk tie purse or case**
84	**Button necklace**
86	**Silk-covered necklace and bangles**
88	**Patches**
90	**Bobble hat and fingerless gloves**

HOME

94	**Button picture**
96	**Silver spoon and fork hooks**
97	**Record bowls**
98	**Decoupage tables**
100	**Cotton reel pin-cushions and jam jar sewing kit**
102	**Owl doorstop**
104	**Dachshund draught excluder**
106	**Paper pattern lampshade**
107	**Hot water bottle cover**
108	**Secret compartment book**
109	**Covered notebooks**
110	**Knitted t-shirt rug**
112	**Cards for all occasions**
114	**Christmas decorations**
118	**Templates**
128	**Acknowledgements**

Toys

A pile of bargain basement acrylic jumpers in different colours was the starting point for our soft toys. Their colours and textures sparked ideas for transformation.

Cuddly
penguin
p.25

Whale
p.24

Whale

The idea for these whales came from the colours of the jumpers we found. You will only need the lower part of a sleeve for each one so there will be plenty of leftovers for other projects. If you are making the whale for a baby or a small child, it is best to embroider the eyes instead of sewing on buttons which might come off and get swallowed after persistent hugging. There is very little sewing here – and it's actually best to do it by hand, so it's a great project to do with children.

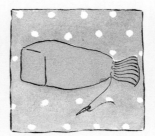

Step 1 The whale is a tube with a flap for the face. The sides of the square flap need to be ¼ of the width of the tube. The easiest way to do it is to turn the jumper inside out and cut off the sleeve. The cuff will be the tail. Draw a line across the sleeve at its widest point (here 16cm/6½in across). Measure 8cm/3¼in up and draw a straight line across at right angles – towards the armhole. This is the bottom of the square. Draw an 8-cm/3¼-in vertical line 8cm/3¼in up and another horizontal line back towards the cuff end. Flip the sleeve over and join the line back to seam. Cut out.

Step 2 Fold the square flap over and pin to the sides. Sew around the three edges with back stitch.

Step 3 Turn the right way round and stuff. Thread a needle with strong sewing or embroidery thread and sew a gathering line all the way across the cuff and pull tight. Make several stitches on the spot to stop this thread unravelling.

Step 4 Cut 2 trapezium shapes (a triangle with the top sliced off) from spare jumper leftovers, preferably the ribbing from the cuffs, and sew on to the body of the whale. Sew on 2 buttons or poppers for eyes, or, if making for a child under three, embroider them on.

See templates
p.118

Cuddly penguin

Looking at the sleeve of a black acrylic jumper, it was just asking to be turned into a cute little cuddly penguin. This is such a simple project that it would be a good one to do with a child – both my children made one with Alfie declaring it his very favourite toy. We used scraps of felt for the features but you could use any bits of fabric. The eyes were made of two buttons, but if the new owner is a very small child it's probably best to embroider eyes, or sew on small bits of fabric.

You will need

- Sleeve from an old jumper
- Scraps of felt or fabric
- 2 buttons for eyes
- Stuffing or finely cut-up old socks

Tools

- Sewing kit

Step 1 Use the whole width of sleeve so you only have to sew the top and bottom. With the sleeve inside out, measure across the width to find a place where it measures about 14cm/5¾in. Draw a straight line across, then measure up about 19cm/7½in and draw a rounded arch shape at the top. Cut across the bottom and around the top, about 1.5cm/½in away from the drawn line.

Step 2 Using a couple of pins to hold in place, sew around the top with the embroidery thread, using back stitch.

Step 3 Turn the right way round and stuff your penguin. Turn the bottom edges in and sew using an over and over stitch almost to the end. Do some final stuffing, particularly in the bottom corners, before closing completely.

Step 4 Cut out a white chest (see template p.118), a beak, flippers and feet from scraps of felt. Sew these on, together with 2 button or fabric eyes.

See templates p.119

Frog

This frog is far more likely to attract princess kisses than the shapeless green jumper it sprang from. I made him one long afternoon in a hospital waiting room. I cut the pattern from an old newspaper and as I didn't have my sewing machine, I hand sewed all the pieces. You could, of course, speed things up with a sewing machine.

You will need
- Large acrylic jumper
- 2 buttons or large poppers for eyes
- Stuffing or finely cut-up old socks

Tools
- Sewing kit

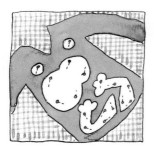

Step 1 Trace, enlarge and cut out pattern pieces. Turn the jumper inside out. Making sure both sides are completely flat, pin on the patterns (through both front and back). Cut out through both thicknesses of jumper so you have 2 of each shape.

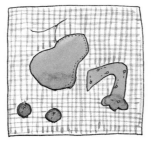

Step 2 Remove paper patterns and re-pin each pair of shapes. Sew a 1-cm/½-in hem around the body leaving a 5-cm/2-in gap at the back. If you are hand sewing use back stitch. Turn inside out and stuff with wadding or fabric scraps. Turn in the edges of the gap and hand sew closed.

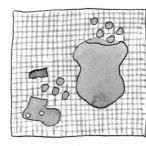

Step 3 Sew and stuff the front and back legs. Pin to body and then, when you are happy with their position, stitch them on.

Step 4 Sew and stuff the eyes and stitch to the top of the head. Sew on buttons or large poppers for eyes.

Pig

With a pig-mad daughter what else could a pink jumper sleeve left over from the patchwork blanket on p.40 be transformed into? A very simple project; Flossie was suitably pleased.

Cut the sleeve off a pink jumper about 25cm/10in up from the cuff. About 2cm/¾in from the edge of the cuff tie a piece of embroidery thread tightly around – this will create the snout. Stuff the rest of the pig until it is nice and fat, fold in the ends and hand sew closed. Cut a circle of felt or fabric and sew on for the end of the snout. Cut out two ear shapes and sew these on, and add two button eyes. Sew a few stitches to create feet and add a strip of fabric for a curly tail.

See templates
p.118

Kitten •

Trace and enlarge the template. Cut two of each shape from a jumper. Pin right sides together and sew a 1-cm/½-in seam around head and body using back stitch. Leave a small gap to stuff. Turn the right way round, stuff and sew closed. Embroider features, sew head to body.

Dodos
p.42

Patchwork
baby blanket
p.40

Fabric-
covered album
p.109

Baby stuff

Lots of these projects would make great presents,
particularly for new parents and babies. If you are
intending to give anything to very young children
think about how it will be used. Make sure that all
small parts are extremely well sewn on and cannot
be pulled off and swallowed. Embroider eyes on
soft toys – rather than sewing on buttons – and
make sure that no stuffing will escape.

Baby bird mobile •

See templates
pp.120-21

You will need

- Small pieces of patterned fabric – shirt scraps are ideal
- Buttons (cut them off the shirts)
- Embroidery thread
- Ribbon, or wool, or string
- 2 garden canes or bamboo sticks

Tools

- Sewing kit

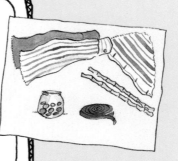

We made this mobile with lots of different pieces of shirt fabric left over from the cushions on p.58 and bunting on p.60. The shapes are simple to cut out and easy to sew – in fact it actually looks nicest if you hand sew the birds. It's a lovely present for a small child or a new baby and as it's so simple it would also be an ideal project to do with children.

Step 1 Trace the bird and heart patterns from the template. Cut out and pin on 2 thicknesses of fabric. Cut out fabric pieces. Repeat so you have 8 pairs of fabric birds, 16 wings and 2 hearts.

Step 2 Pin pairs of fabric birds and wings together and sew all the way round 5mm/¼in from the edge. Don't worry if they fray – this is part of the charm. Stop just before reaching the starting point leaving an opening for stuffing. Stuff and finish sewing all the way round.

Step 3 Sew on button eyes. If you want to embroider a name or a date on the heart, do this on one piece of fabric before stitching to the other, and then stuff and finish as in step 2.

Step 4 Cut four 50-cm/20-in lengths of narrow ribbon, string, wool or strong thread. Cut four 70-cm/ 27-in lengths and one 30-cm/12-in length. Sew the shortest piece of ribbon to the heart and the longer lengths to the birds.

Step 5 Place the garden canes in a cross and bind together with wool, ribbon, string or cotton. Tie the heart to the middle cross. Tie the birds on shorter ribbons to the ends of the canes. Tie the longer-ribboned birds to the middle of the canes.

◀ **Step 6** Tie one more long piece of ribbon (or wool or string) to the middle of the cross to attach the mobile to ceiling.

Baby hat, mittens and booties

See templates p.118

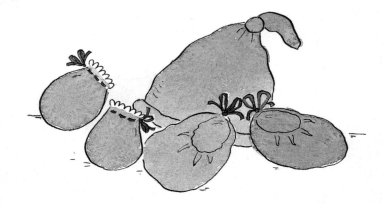

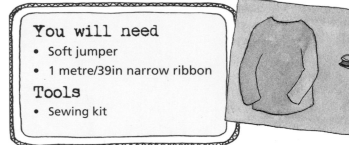

You will need
- Soft jumper
- 1 metre/39in narrow ribbon

Tools
- Sewing kit

This lovely set for a newborn baby was made from a really soft acrylic mix (and therefore washable) jumper. A soft stretchy fleece would be a good alternative. It is very simple and quick to hand or machine sew and would make a great present. The sizes here fit a newborn baby, but 6-month-old Howie squeezed into it for the photograph. We trimmed the mittens with some lace which was already on the jumper, but you could use contrasting lace or ribbon, or just leave them plain.

HAT Step 1 Cut one of the sleeves off, and measure across to find a place where it is about 17cm/6½in wide, near the top of the sleeve. Measure down 40cm/16in and cut off. The wide part of the sleeve is the bottom of the hat. Turn the sleeve inside out. You want to create a very long thin triangle at the top, so measure about 18cm/7in from the bottom up each side, and from these points, draw a diagonal line to the middle of the very top to create a point. Sew along these lines, then cut off the excess.

Step 2 Turn it the right way round, and fold up 1.5cm/½in twice at the bottom of the hat. Put a few stitches to hold in place, but don't sew all the way round as this will stop it being so stretchy. Tie a knot in the top.

MITTENS Using the egg cosy template, cut out 2 pieces for each mitten and sew together using back stitch. Turn them the right way round. We trimmed the edge of the mittens with lace. Thread a big-eyed needle with some narrow ribbon and do a gathering stitch around the bottom of the mitten, about 1cm/½in from the edge. This can be then tied in a bow to hold the mitten in place on the baby's hand.

BOOTIES Step 1 Draw an oval, approximately 25cm/10in in length, and 21cm/8¼in wide. Fold in half lengthways and measure 8cm/3¼in along the fold from one end. From this point, draw a line out to the edge at an angle of 45 degrees. Sew along this line, and trim off the excess.

Step 2 Fold over a 1-cm/½-in seam all the way around and sew, leaving a gap near the seam to thread the ribbon through. Cut a smaller oval of felt about 9cm/3½in x 6cm/2½in and sew this in the middle of the bootee, on the underside. Now thread the ribbon through the channel you have created. Put the bootee on the baby's foot and tie the ribbon at the back.

Baby bag and play mat

You will need

- Old curtains, preferably with lining
- About 1 metre/39in square of plastic fabric
- 6 metres/20ft of strong webbing tape, at least 4cm/1½in wide

Tools

- Sewing kit
- Sewing machine

Any parent of a baby or toddler will know how much stuff you have to carry around – food, toys, spare clothes, nappies... the list is endless. What you need is a simple, strong bag big enough to hold absolutely everything. A tough play mat that can double up as a changing mat or picnic rug is another essential. Old curtains are ideal as the fabric is usually much more substantial than dress-making fabric. Lining the mat with plastic tablecloth material makes it waterproof too. This one rolls up and is attached to the outside of the bag with ties made from cotton webbing tape in a contrasting colour.

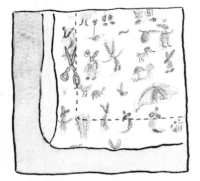

BAG Step 1 Fold one curtain in half, right sides together. Draw a rectangle on it, approximately 60cm/24in x 50cm/20in, but make it as big as you like. Make the two bottom corners rounded. Pin and cut out the fabric and lining together. 60cm/24in is for the height of the bag, and 50cm/20in for the width.

Step 2 Measure round 3 edges of your rectangle, and cut a strip of fabric and lining which is the same length. You may have to sew 2 pieces of fabric together. This will be a gusset for the bag. Pin (right sides together) and machine sew the strip to one rectangle and then the other with a 1.5-cm/½-in seam allowance.

Step 3 Turn the top edge over twice, about 5cm/2in each time. Press with an iron and then top stitch. Cut 2 strips of fabric for the handles, about 12cm/5in wide and as long as you want. Press them in half lengthways, folding the raw edges in and top-stitch. Sew to the top of the bag. We also added a pocket to the front of our bag.

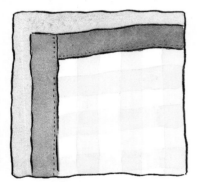

BLANKET Step 4 We made the play mat from the other curtain. Cut two squares of equal size, one from the curtain and one from the plastic fabric. Ours is about 1 metre/39in square, but you can make it any size you like. Lay them both together on the floor, wrong sides together, and pin or tack around the edges to hold in place. Press your webbing tape in half, and fold this over the raw edges of the mat. Pin to hold in place, then machine sew all the way round.

Step 5 Add some strips of webbing tape to your bag so you can roll up your rug and tie it on to the bag.

Baby hat, mittens
and booties
p.34

Baby bag and
play mat
p.36

We made this bag and matching play mat from a pair of children's curtains originally from the Queen Elizabeth Children's Hospital in Hackney, London. After treating children for more than 100 years it finally closed down in 1996. The last doctors and nurses transferred to The Royal London Hospital and these curtains ended up in a local charity shop. Howie's hat came from the sleeve of a soft red cardigan and the mittens and booties were made from the rest.

Patchwork baby blanket

You will need
- 3 jumpers in contrasting colours
- Cotton fabric or bias binding

Tools
- Sewing kit
- Sewing machine

This beautiful baby blanket was made from three old jumpers. We chose ones which were very soft, but also washable – an important factor when making anything for a baby. We edged the blanket with a strip of Liberty lawn. The underside of the blanket was cut from the back of one of the jumpers, which limited the size. If you want to make a bigger one, back with fabric or fleece. You could also embroider the baby's name and birthdate on it to make it extra special. The Dodos (p.42) were made with leftovers from the same jumpers and we also used a sleeve from the pink jumper to make the pig (p.28), and to cover a photo album (p.127).

Step 1 Cut out a 12-cm/5-in square of cardboard to use as a template. Cut out 8 squares from each jumper.

Step 2 Lay all the squares out on a table and arrange them in a pattern. You need 6 rows of 4 squares.

Step 3 Then, row by row, sew them together, with a seam allowance of 1cm/½in. Press the seams open. Then sew the rows together and press. If you are personalizing with embroidery do this now before attaching the backing.

Step 4 Decide what you want to back the blanket with – either a whole piece of one of the jumpers, or a piece of fabric. Lay the blanket on the backing wrong sides together. Pin and sew around the edge, 1cm/½in in, to hold both pieces together.

Step 5 Now bind the edges. Cut 4 strips of fabric, 8cm/3¼in wide, one for each edge of the blanket. Press them in half, wrong side inside. Lay one of the strips along one of the edges, with right sides together and raw edges matching, and sew 2cm/¾in from the edge. Do the same for all the edges. Then press the fabric over so it covers the edge, and fold the fabric in underneath and tack to hold in place. To make the corners look neat, cut the fabric at one corner flush with the edge, and then cover it with the fabric from the adjoining edge, folding in the raw edges. When you have covered all 4 edges, top stitch from the top side of the blanket, along the inside edge of the fabric to hold everything in place.

Give your blanket a final press to finish and then put it to use keeping a little one warm and cosy.

Dodos

See templates p.123

You will need

- Soft jersey material – we used lambswool, angora and cashmere mix jumpers
- Cotton fabric or bias binding
- Stuffing or cut-up old socks
- Strong thread
- Embroidery thread

Tools

- Sewing kit

My younger son, Oliver, was born in France and among the traditional teddies given by friends and neighbours were these little 'hankerchief' soft toys. I had never seen them before (although I think they are now quite popular) and we always called them Dodos – the French word for the kind of small cuddly toys children take to bed with them. I guess it must come from the French verb for sleep, *dormir*, and it seems to be spelt in a number of different ways. They are a really tactile combination of soft toy and blanket and are perfect for tiny fingers.

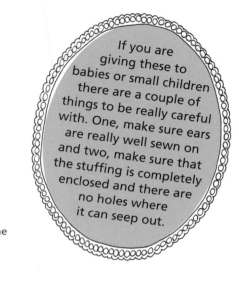

Step 1 Cut a square of the size you want your dodo to be. Ours range between 20cm/8in to 28cm/11in square. On the wrong side of the square, draw a circle in the middle with a diameter of between 10cm/4in and 12cm/5in. A large mug or jam jar is about the right size.

Step 2 Using strong thread, sew a gathering stitch all the way round the circle line, leaving a long tail at the start and the end.

If you are giving these to babies or small children there are a couple of things to be really careful with. One, make sure ears are really well sewn on and two, make sure that the stuffing is completely enclosed and there are no holes where it can seep out.

Step 3 Gently pull both ends of the thread to create a little pouch. As you draw the edges closer, push the stuffing into the pouch to create the head. Keep stuffing until it is nice and round and keep drawing the gathering threads till they are as tight as they will go without breaking. Either tie the thread or sew both ends back into the fabric to secure the gathering.

Step 4 You will probably still have a small gap, which must be closed. Either sew a small circle of fabric over the hole, or machine or hand sew a line beneath the head – where the neck would be if the dodo had a neck!

Step 5 Cut out 4 ear shapes from the template. Pin each pair, right sides together and hand sew around the curved edge using back stitch. Turn them the right way round and sew securely to the head. Embroider eyes, nose and mouth detail on to the face. For some reason they seem to work best with very little detail – just two curves for closed eyes looks fine. (See pp.30–31 for different versions.) Either hem or bind the raw edges with bias binding or a strip of fabric.

Family

Making stuff for children or with children has always been one of the reasons for craft. Home-made doll's houses, rocking horses, peg dolls and rag dolls used to be the mainstay of the nursery. Don't think that because the children you know seem to spend hours glued to a screen that they won't appreciate a handmade toy, or making one with you. Our children have scrapped for ownership over all the animals in this book and have even made some of their own. They also loved making the lego clock, record bowls, glitter cups and button pictures.

Lego clock p.51

Frilly pinny p.46

Children's chef's hat p.48

Cook's apron p.42

Children's apron p.49

Frilly pinny

The aprons on these and the following pages make the most of their original source; a man's cotton shirt. The back panel becomes the apron skirt, the strip with the buttons on becomes the waistband of the frilly pinny, the buttonhole strip makes an adjustable strap on the cook's apron, and the collar becomes the headband for the child-sized chef's hat.

You will need
- Large shirt

Tools
- Sewing kit
- Sewing machine

Step 1 Cut up the shirt – separate the back panel up to the collar, front panels and the sleeves. Slice off the cuffs and open up each sleeve along the seam. Measure 50cm/20in from the bottom edge of the back panel and cut off in a straight line. Measure and calculate the length of bottom plus sides.

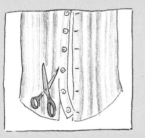

Step 2 Carefully cut off the strips with buttons and buttonholes from the front panels. Divide remaining fabric from the front panels into 6 strips of equal width. Sew 4 together to create one long, thin strip. Press and sew a narrow 5-mm/¼-in hem along one long edge.

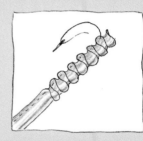

Step 3 Sew a gathering stitch along the other long edge – either by machine or hand. Gently pull the gathering thread until the frill reaches the length measured in step one.

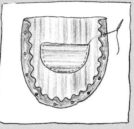

Step 4 Pin the frill to the apron, right sides together, and sew. Iron the frill out. Cut a semi-circle about 30cm/12in wide and 20cm/8in deep from one of the sleeves. Press a hem all the way round. Pin to the centre of the apron and top stitch around 3 sides to create a pocket.

Step 5 Sew the strip with buttons to the top of the apron to create a waist band. Press the remaining 2 strips from the front of the shirts lengthways. Turn edges in and pin. Top stitch and sew to the edge of the waistband to create ties.

Don't forget to save any leftover pieces – perfect for bunting, the baby bird mobile or lavender hearts.

Cook's apron

You will need
- Large shirt

Tools
- Sewing kit

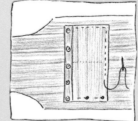

Step 1 Dissect the shirt as for the frilly pinny (p.47). Trim back the panel into a flattened triangle shape and hem the sides and top.

Step 2 Cut a rectangle 20cm/8in x 35cm/15in from the button edge of the shirt front. Press a hem along 3 edges, pin to the apron front and sew with top stitch. Divide the pocket vertically with a line of stitches about 10cm/4in from the edge.

Step 3 Top stitch the long and short edges of the buttonhole strip. Sew one end of strip to the top left-hand side of apron. Sew a shirt button (take one from cuff) to the top inside to make an adjustable neck strap. Make waist ties in the same way as the frilly pinny and sew them on.

Children's chef's hat

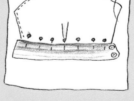

You will need
- Large shirt

Tools
- Sewing kit

Step 1 Use the collar base for the hat band. Open up a sleeve and press flat, measure 25cm/10in down from the top of curve and cut straight across. Press and sew a 5-mm /¼-in hem around the top and sides. Open the seam on top of the collar base and insert raw edge of sleeve. Pin from one side first and then the other, inserting a pleat if necessary. Sew together.

Step 2 Sew a gathering stitch round the top of the sleeve, pull tight and secure.

Step 3 Sew elastic across the back, so it fits easily on the child's head.

Children's aprons

You will need
- For 2 aprons, 1 large shirt plus leftovers from another shirt

Tools
- Sewing kit

Make this in the same way as the cook's apron but scale it down. They can both be made from one shirt – cut one apron from the back panel and one from the front panel with the buttons done up. Use the buttonhole strip or lower part of the collar for the neck band – both button to the top of the apron.

Scrabble magnets

Scrabble tiles, dominoes, and other bits from games can easily be turned into fridge magnets. The best way to do it is with sticky-backed magnetic sheets or tape, available from most craft shops. Cut to size, stick on and think up your best triple-scoring word.

Lego clock

This is a great project to do with children – in fact they'll probably be better at creating the numbers than you. You can buy battery operated clock kits from lots of craft stores. Then it's simply a matter of drilling a small hole in the very centre of a baseboard, attaching the clock bits and getting creative with the numbers.

Tea and egg cosies

See templates p.118 & p.120

You will need

- Chunky woollen jumper
- Scraps of fabric for appliqué shapes
- Narrow ribbon
- Felt

Tools

- Sewing kit
- Needle with an eye big enough to take the ribbon

The insulating qualities of a thick woollen sweater are put to good use here in a tea cosy and matching egg cosies – perfect for lazy weekend breakfasts, or when you're having a cup of tea in the garden.

Blanket stitching the edges with embroidery thread stops them from fraying – but if you can find a sweater that has shrunk in the wash and effectively turned into felt, so much the better. You won't need the whole jumper – the top half of ours was reborn as a waterbottle cover (p.107). Lay the jumper flat on the table. The bottom of the jumper will become the tea cosy and the cuffs will be transformed into two egg cosies.

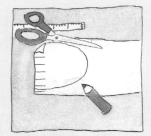

EGG COSY Step 1 Turn the sleeves inside out and pin on the egg cosy template. Draw around, then cut out 2cm/¾in outside drawn line. Pin together and, using a back stitch, sew all the way round the drawn line.

Step 2 Turn the cosy the right way round. Cut a coxcomb and beak from felt or fabric scraps and hand sew them on.

Step 3 Embroider the eyes and say goodbye forever to cold eggs.

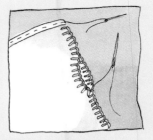

TEA COSY Step 1 Measure round the widest part of your tea pot, not including the handle or the spout, and mark half this length along the bottom of the jumper. Measure how tall you need the cosy, add another 5cm/2in and draw a line across the top. Cut through the back and front of the jumper to give 2 rectangles. Pin these together.

Step 2 Using your teapot as a guide, mark a space on each short edge for the handle and spout. Hand sew the side seams together with embroidery thread using blanket stitch. When you reach the handle and spout marks, make a few stitches on the spot to stop the thread unravelling, and cut off.

Step 3 Sew blanket stitch around each hole. Along the top raw edge turn over a 5-mm/¼-in hem and sew with running stitch all around the top.

Step 4 Decorate the front with appliqué shapes cut from the templates. Use felt or other scraps of fabric and sew on with embroidery thread. Thread a needle with narrow ribbon, and starting at the handle side make 1-cm/½-in stitches about 3cm/1¼in below the top edge all the way round. Pull the ribbon tight to gather the top together and tie in a bow. Enjoy a lovely hot cup of tea!

No-sew balaclava

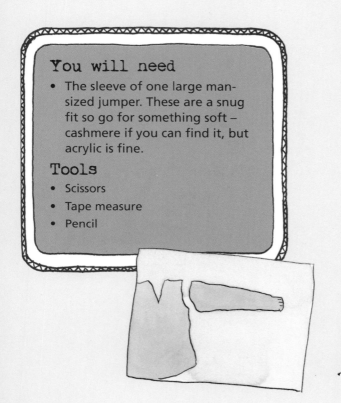

You will need
- The sleeve of one large man-sized jumper. These are a snug fit so go for something soft – cashmere if you can find it, but acrylic is fine.

Tools
- Scissors
- Tape measure
- Pencil

I made these for Isaac and Oliver one freezing February morning at 8.55 when I realized they'd lost their umpteenth hats of the winter. I sliced the sleeves off a moth-eaten jumper, chopped a couple of face-sized holes out and tied a knot at the top. I intended to neaten up the holes and hem the edges when they got home from school but I never quite got round to it.

Fancy balaclava (with sewing)

Of course you could make this much neater and warmer by combining two sleeves – either from the same jumper or two contrasting colours. In which case, follow through to step 3. Then pin the sleeves right sides together and sew most of the way round the face opening. Turn the right way round and finish off the face seam. Hem the bottom edges and sew together. Instead of a knot in the top, sew a gathering thread through the two thicknesses and pull tight.

Step 1 Carefully cut the sleeve off a jumper along the seam that joins it to the shoulder.

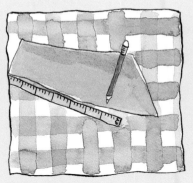

Step 2 Lay it out flat and, from the bottom of the longest edge (where it joined the shoulder), mark up about 15cm/6in. Then mark another 12cm/5in up.

Step 3 Draw a shallow spoon-shaped hole between the two points. It may look small but it will stretch and you can always make it bigger if necessary. Cut out the scoop.

Step 4 If the balaclava wearer is nearby get them to try it on and adjust the face opening accordingly. If not don't worry, you can always do it later.

Step 5 If you want a pom-pom on the top, make a series of vertical cuts all around the cuff edge about 8cm/3¼in long and 1cm/½in apart. If you don't want a pom-pom (my sons didn't) just go straight to the knot – tie it about 8cm/3¼in or 9cm/3½in from the cuff end.

Hoodlets

See templates pp.122-3

You will need

- 1 sweatshirt or fleece
- Scrap of felt or contrasting material for inner ears

Tools

- Sewing kit
- Glue

These animal hoodlets are based on one of the first things we ever made at Buttonbag. They are very simple and can be hand sewn in less than an hour. An old sweatshirt or fleece is ideal because it's soft and cosy and doesn't fray. The basic shape is the same for all the animals – just add different shaped ears to turn them into mice, sheep, cats, bunnies, bears, rabbits, monkeys, etc. They are fun to wear and warm, great for Halloween and can be adapted for last-minute nativity plays. Let's say if you ever, at short notice, have to provide a costume for third sheep from the left.

FROM LEFT TO RIGHT
Isaac (now 11), Alfred (now 9), Flossie (now 7) and Oliver (now 8)

Step 1 Trace the template, enlarge to A3 size and cut out. Lay sweatshirt out flat with fluffy side on the inside and pin main pattern and ears (or spikes) on. Cut out 2 through both thicknesses.

Step 2 For all animals apart from the dragon, remove the paper pattern and pin together the big curved seam and the short straight seam. Either hand or machine sew together.

Step 3 Remove the pins and use scissors to make a series of small snips around the outer curve. This helps the hoodlet fit properly. Turn it so the fluffy side is outside.

Step 4 Cut out inner ears from felt or fabric scraps and glue to the fleecy ears. Pinch the bottom of each ear in half and sew a couple of stitches to hold in place. This makes the ears stand up slightly.

Step 5 Try on child – you may need to adjust the short straight seam under the chin. Position and pin the ears. Take the hoodlet off and hand sew the ears on.

FOR THE DRAGON ONLY
After step 1, remove the paper pattern and pin both spikes to the fluffy side of one hoodlet, spikes pointing inwards. Use the pins to shape the spikes to fit the curve. Pin the other hoodlet shape on top, fluffy side inwards.

Hand or machine sew together. Remove the pins and turn the right way round. You can adjust the short straight seam under the chin if necessary.

Bears and monkeys have the same ear shapes – but bear ears look best on top of the head and monkey ears seem more monkeyish at the side, more or less where your ears would go!

Shirt cushions

Men's stripey shirts can be easily transformed into surprisingly stylish cushions with an air of summery seaside homes about them (as long as you've washed them first). You can of course use any largish shirt. Turn the buttoned shirt inside out, and lay flat on a table. Measure your cushion pad and draw a square on the shirt of the same dimensions plus 1cm/½in. Cut out, pin and sew all the way round. Trim seams, undo buttons, turn through and press. Put in the cushion pad and button up. Simple and effective!

Bunting •

You will need
- 1 man's cotton shirt for every 2 metres/7ft of bunting
- Cotton tape, ribbon or bias binding

Tools
- Ruler
- Sewing kit
- Sewing machine

Men's cotton shirts make brilliant bunting. Choose two or more shirts with contrasting patterns – stripes, checks, gingham, polka dots or paisley. This is where the larger gentleman comes into his own – the bigger the man, the bigger the shirt, which means more fabric for your flags.

This project is for double-sided bunting and, while it is very simple, it is much easier if you can use a sewing machine. If you want to hand sew, it might be best to make one-sided bunting which still looks lovely hanging in your garden. Make the bunting in exactly the same way, just skip step 3.

Step 1 Make a triangle template approximately 15cm/6in x 25cm/10in out of thin cardboard – cereal boxes are ideal.

Step 2 Dissect the shirt. Open all the seams so you have as much fabric as possible ready to use.

For ribbon or cotton tape: follow step 5, or simply pin the triangles to the tape and machine sew them on. This is quick but doesn't give such a professional finish.

Step 3 Lay the pieces flat on a table. Use your template to draw as many triangles as possible. Don't worry if some are pointing in different directions – this creates the illusion of lots of contrasting fabric. Cut out all triangles. Repeat for all shirts.

Step 4 Pin contrasting fabric triangles right sides together. Machine sew the 2 long edges. Trim the point and turn the right way round. Iron flat if necessary. Skip this step if you are hand sewing. (Unless you are a complete hand sewing fanatic, it's best to use single-sided flags with no hems – it doesn't fray too much and you get twice as many flags!)

Step 5 Fold the bias binding in half lengthways, sandwiching the short edge of each triangle in the fold as you go. It really helps to iron a very defined crease down the centre of the entire length of bias binding before you start. Secure each flag with a pin and machine sew. Don't forget to leave at least a metre/39 inches at each end to secure the bunting.

Deckchairs

These deckchairs were tatty but unbroken and quickly brought back to glory with a bit of sandpaper, paint and new seat covers. After sanding down and repainting the wooden frames, we carefully removed the old seats and used them as patterns to make exact copies from a fabulous sixties curtain and an African wrap. Although the fabric was quite robust we doubled it up to make it even stronger. We re-attached the seats to the frames using the original dome-headed tacks.

Beach bag

Just the thing for carrying a book and swimming stuff to the beach, our simple-to-sew beach bag was made using an old, bright orange, flowery 1970s curtain – we used the rest to cover the deckchair on p.62. The handles were bought from a craft shop, and we chose wooden ones to complement the fabric. The bag looks nicer if it is lined, either with the same fabric, or a contrasting one – we used some plain orange cotton.

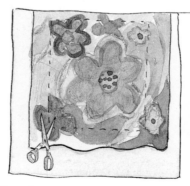

Step 1 Fold the fabric in half with the right side inside and lay flat. Draw a rectangle approximately 60cm/24in x 45cm/18in.

Step 2 Using a curve shape to draw round (such as the actual bag handles), draw a concave curve at the top two corners, and a smaller convex curve at the bottom two corners. Pin together and cut out about 2cm/¾in outside the line. Fold the lining fabric in half, lay the cut out bag piece on top, and cut out 2 lining pieces the same size.

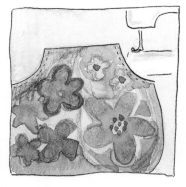

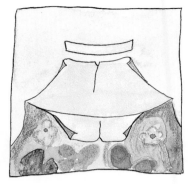

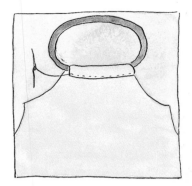

Step 3 With right sides together, machine sew both the lining and the main fabric down the sides and along the bottom. Turn the main fabric the right way round and press a 1.5cm/½in hem along the curved side pieces. Do the same to the lining, but keep the right side on the inside, and press the hem to the outside. Insert the lining fabric into the bag, and pin and topstitch the newly-pressed curved edges together.

Step 4 The top edges of the bag will probably be wider than your handles, so make an inverted pleat by marking where the middle is, and folding the fabric in from each side to the middle, until it measures the same length as the handle. Pin, and then sew on a piece of webbing tape to the top edge.

Step 5 Place the handle on the top edge of the bag, and fold the tape over and stitch down to hold the handle in place. Repeat for the other handle.

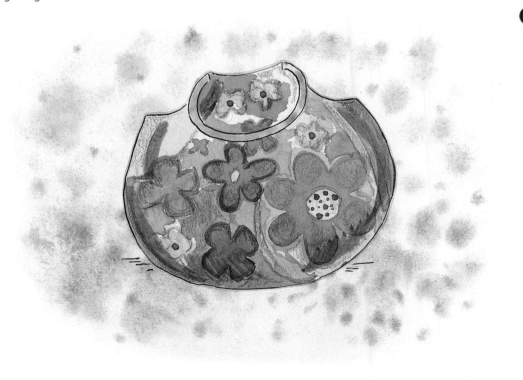

Jam jar candles •

Once we'd cut away the discoloured part of the smaller deckchair seat (p.62) we were left with a piece of tough, woven nylon fabric whose stripes were evocative of all things good and summery. Too good to waste, we cut it up and sewed simple sleeves to fit around different width jam jars. A nightlight in each and you've got perfect garden candles. This would work with any vibrantly coloured fabric.

Glitter cup candles •

Single cup and saucers make great tealight candle holders. Stick the cup to the saucer with a strong craft glue. Paint the entire inside of the cup with a thin layer of PVA glue. Tip in glitter – the finer the better. Roll it round and then gently tap out the excess. When dry you might need to fill in any bare patches.

Friends

A handmade purse or necklace is a great present to give to a friend. After all you can never have too many beautiful bags, purses or baubles. Our favourites include the silk-wrapped bangles, toy box jewellery and silk tie purses. All dead easy and achievable by even the most inexperienced crafter. If you are pretty confident with a needle try the Kelly bag or the satchel, both are fashioned from suit jackets incorporating the pockets, buttonholes and lining.

Bobble hat p.90

Toy box jewellery p.70

Silk-covered necklace and bangles p.86

Patches p.88

Button
necklace p.84

Tweedy
satchel p.72

Fingerless
gloves p.90

Old book handbag

You will need
- Old hardback book
- Fabric for the end and lining pieces
- Bag handles and ribbon
- Magnetic clasp
- Strong PVA or fabric glue

Tools
- Scalpel or craft knife
- Sewing kit

We made our handbag with an old Beano annual (from 1978 – Dan thought it was sacrilege!) but of course you could use any old hardback book. You will only need the cover for the bag but don't throw the pages away – see the decoupage project (pp.98–9) and greetings cards (p.112). Choose a strong fabric for the end pieces and a contrasting fabric for the lining – we used corduroy and green gingham. This bag isn't supposed to be for carrying around everything but the kitchen sink, it's more of an evening bag for your phone and lipstick. You can find bag handles and magnetic clasps at good haberdashery shops or online.

Step 1 Using a craft knife or scalpel carefully cut out the pages from the book.

Step 2 Open the book out to about 15cm/6in, stand on the end fabric, and mark out a triangle shape. Cut 2 of these shapes, with about 1.5cm/½in extra all around, from both the end fabric and the lining fabric. Using some strong PVA or fabric glue, glue one edge of end fabric down one side of book, then glue the other side. The edge of the fabric should protrude about 1.5cm/½in above the top of the book.

Step 3 Attach the handles before lining. We used black plastic handles which had holes at each end and attached them to the inside of the book cover by threading a short piece of ribbon through each one and securing with strong glue.

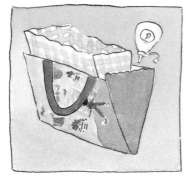

Step 4 Cut 2 rectangles the same size as the book cover out of lining fabric, plus a seam allowance of 1.5cm/½in. Sew these pieces together with the lining triangles so they are same shape as the book. Put the lining in the bag, fold the top edges in and glue all around to hold in place.

Step 5 Glue a magnetic clasp on to the inside top edges. Alternatively you could glue on 2 pieces of ribbon to act as ties.

Tweedy satchel

You will need
- Tweed jacket
- Belt

Tools
- Tailor's chalk
- Leather punch or nail
- Sewing kit
- Sewing machine

The best thing about a well-made jacket is the pockets. Especially men's jackets. This lovely tweedy number has five; two placket pockets at the front, one breast pocket for your handkerchief and two on the inside for wallets and letters and stuff. This satchel makes the most of one of the front pockets and we also used the buttonholes and buttons to make the fastenings. If the jacket is lined, like this one, you can also incorporate that into the bag. An old leather belt makes an adjustable strap.

facing

front

back

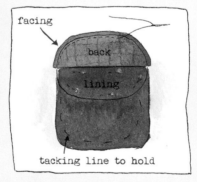

facing

back

lining

tacking line to hold

trim and hem gusset

fold top of lining and tweed over and hem

Step 1 Draw paper patterns for the front, back and facing, making them the size you want and roughly the same shape as in the illustration. Pin the front pattern on the jacket, centered over the pocket. Draw around with tailor's chalk or pencil. Remove the patterns but put the pins back into the fabric of the front and back pieces, just inside the drawn lines, to keep all the layers of fabric together. Cut out pieces through all thicknesses of fabric; tweed and lining, making sure you keep the pocket in one piece.

Step 2 On the back piece, fold down the top quarter of lining (it was about 12cm/5in for us) and pin. Tack the bottom half of the lining to the fabric. Pin the facing to the top of the back, right sides together. Sew across top and sides. Notch curves and turn the right way round and top stitch. Now fold the lining back over the raw edge of the facing and hand sew down, folding in a neat hem.

Step 3 Cut a long thin strip from the jacket to be the gusset. It needs to be as long as the sides and bottom of the front of the satchel plus a little bit more for hemming. We made ours 82cm/32¼in x 10cm/4in. You may need to join 2 pieces together. Pin the gusset to the front, right sides together, and sew. Sew through the lining too. Fold the top of the front lining and tweed fabric over, creating a 1-cm/½-in hem and sew. Trim and hem the gusset if necessary. Stitch gusset to the back, right sides together. Notch curves and turn the satchel right way round.

  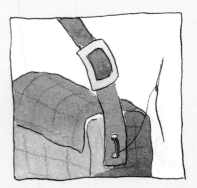

Step 4 To make the straps, cut 2 strips from the jacket front 6cm/2½in wide and 10cm/4in long incorporating buttonholes, and top stitch all edges.

Step 5 Sew the straps to the satchel flap and mark where buttons will go. On ours, it was just below the pocket placket. Sew on buttons.

Step 6 Buckle the belt and cut about 30cm/12in below the buckle. Make 2 holes in the cut ends using a leather punch or a nail. Sew in place.

Kelly bag

You will need
- Suit jacket with a pocket
- Bag handle
- Big popper fastener

Tools
- Sewing kit
- Sewing machine

This is the kind of bag you can imagine Grace Kelly swinging along the Riviera. Our bag is made from a gentleman's dark grey pinstripe suit jacket. Maybe it belonged to Cary Grant. We used the pocket as a feature on the outside of the bag, and finished it off with a plastic handle and a sparkly brooch. The bag is lined using the lining from the suit. It would also work well with a contrasting fabric.

Step 1 Lay the jacket flat on the table, draw a trapezium shape, about 18cm/7in at the top, 30cm/12in at the bottom and 23cm/9in high. Make sure the top is about 3cm/1¼in above the pocket. Pin the front of the jacket to the back and cut out both pieces together with lining, leaving a 2-cm/¾-in seam allowance.

Step 2 Unpin and tack the lining to the back and front pieces. Put 2 pieces right sides together, pin, and machine sew with a 2-cm/¾-in seam allowance, down the sides and along the bottom. Press seams open.

Step 3 To make a flat bottom you need to create a gusset along the bottom seam. Squash each corner down matching bottom seam against side seam – it should look like triangle. Pin. Draw a straight line across, about 5cm/2in from the point of the triangle. Sew. Turn the bag the right way round.

Step 4 Turn down the top and press along the drawn line. Fold the lining in and hand stitch. Sew on a big popper to close the bag and a handle to hold.

See templates p.120

Fabric flower corsage •

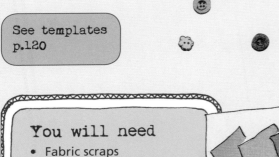

You will need
- Fabric scraps
- Ribbon (optional)
- Button (optional)
- Safety pin

Tools
- Sewing kit

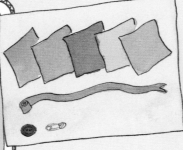

This is a very effective way of creating a corsage from small scraps of fabric. You need a minimum of six flower shapes, one for the base and five for the petals but you can make them fuller by adding more petals. Adding a ribbon gives the corsage a rosette feel – great if you have any political or pony club events coming up!

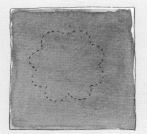

Step 1 Trace and cut out the flower template. Pin on to the fabric and cut out at least 6 shapes – 5 for petals and 1 for the base.

Step 2 Fold one flower shape in half and half again so it looks like a heart and sew to the middle of the base flower.

Step 3 Repeat with the remaining petal shapes. Fluff up the petals when you've finished to make the flower fuller.

Step 4 Sew a button in the centre. Fold over and sew ribbon to the back if you're making a rosette and add a safety pin or brooch.

You can make these from felt, denim, tweed, t-shirt fabric, tartan, silk, scraps of acrylic jumpers – even the pages from old books. Try Mills & Boon novels – perfect for Valentine's day.

Toy box jewellery •

Monopoly houses, toy soldiers, plastic animals, scrabble tiles, dice and Barbie accessories all become miniature objects of art when hanging from a chain or an earring. Our best source (apart from our children's bedrooms) was a compendium of miniature games full of tiny playing cards, chess pieces, dominoes and dice. Second-hand shops are also good places to find chains and bracelets to attach them to and new jewellery fixings are cheaply and easily available online or from jewellery-making supply shops. A pair of thin-nosed jewellery pliers is also useful.

MAKING A HOLE

Method 1 Use an electric drill with a 1.5-mm drill bit. For safety, hold the piece you are drilling still by pushing it into plasticine or taping it to a board with masking tape.

Method 2 Push a needle into a wine cork to make a handle. Light a candle. Heat the tip of the needle in the flame for a few seconds. Carefully and quickly push it through the plastic. This doesn't work for metal monopoly pieces.

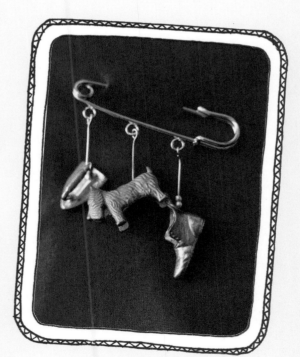

Granny purse

See templates p.124

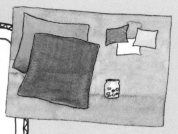

You will need
- Fabric – try denim, wool or floral fabric
- Popper fastener
- Bias binding
- Buttons, ribbon, and other fabric scraps for decoration.

Tools
- Sewing kit

Use the simple pear-shape template to make fabulous granny purses out of all kinds of fabric. We kept the basic purse really simple and then jazzed them up with fun decorations, inspired by some of our favourite Buttonbag kits. If you are feeling more adventurous you can use the same pattern to make a clasp-frame purse. You will need to buy the frame from a craft shop. However, it takes quite a bit of patience to poke the fabric into the jaws of the frame (and a very strong fabric glue), and you may well decide you like the easy version best!

Step 1 Trace and cut out the pattern template. Enlarge to desired size. Pin to your fabric and cut out 2 shapes for each purse. If you want to add a lining cut out 2 more from a contrasting fabric. Cut the top off 1 shape (and also 1 lining if you are using).

Step 2 Pin purse shapes right sides together and sew around the curved edge using back stitch. Repeat for the lining if using. Pin lining and purse fabric right sides together and sew around the top edge of the flap and most of the straight edge leaving a gap big enough to turn it through to the right way round. Turn it through and hand sew the gap closed.

Step 3 Unleash your creative imagination on decorations. Use the kitten head template and add a silk tie bow, a felt puppy, an embroidered flower or buttons.... Sew on a popper to finish.

Step 4 If you aren't using a lining, turn the purse the right way round and finish the open edges with bias binding or a strip of fabric. We made ours from a strip of silk tie – they are usually cut on the bias and therefore perfect for bias-binding.

Envelope purses and bags .

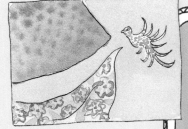

These are the easiest purses ever – make them big enough and from a fairly stiff fabric and they make great clutch bags. Like the granny purses, the thing that makes these stand out is the decoration – if you don't have time to get fancy, finish with a fabulous brooch. A glittery trinket that's been lying unloved in your granny's jewellery box or a dusty corner of the charity shop will transform this into a fantastic evening bag.

You will need
- Fabric – we used an old blanket
- Lining fabric – try a silk scarf
- Popper fastener
- Decoration – more fabric scraps or a diamanté brooch

Tools
- Sewing kit

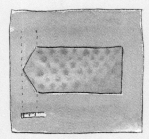

Step 1 Cut an oblong of fabric about 20cm/8in x 36cm/15¼in. Measure and cut a shallow point along one short edge. Cut the same from lining fabric.

Step 2 Pin the 2 pieces right sides together and sew all the way round using back stitch. Leave a gap along one long edge, just big enough to turn purse the right way. Trim the corners and turn through. Press flat and hand sew the gap closed.

Step 3 Fold the bottom third up and pin. Hand stitch the two side seams using a tiny over and over stitch. Sew on a popper.

Step 4 Pin on the biggest, most glittery brooch you can find and prepare to party.

Silk tie purse or case •

Silk ties make luxurious cases for all kinds of objects that are usually lying around loose in your bag or coat pocket; sunglasses, i-pods, mobile phones, pencils, make-up or money. The brilliant thing about them is that most ties have a very fine, soft, woollen inner layer so your cases are naturally padded – perfect for fragile glasses or techie things. The cases are closed with a popper, but you can add a button or decorate with a sparkly brooch – the kind you can always find in a second-hand shop.

The narrow end can be used in exactly the same way to make a lipstick purse or a case for say, a beautiful pen.

Step 1 From the wide end of the tie, measure and cut: for a sunglasses or pencil case you will need 45cm/18in; for a phone or i-pod case 38cm/15in; for a little money purse, 22cm/8¾in. For a lipstick case, measure 20cm/8in from the narrow end of the tie and make in exactly the same way.

Step 2 Look at the cut end. You will see an inner layer of light wadding. Loosen the silk and cut off about 2cm/¾in of wadding. Now fold the fabric in to make a neat hem.

Step 3 Pin and sew across the top with a simple over and over stitch. If the seam down the centre of the tie is coming apart – it happens sometimes – stitch it closed. Now's a good time to unpick any labels or little strips (sometimes sewn on to the back so a gent can tuck the narrow end in to look all tidy).

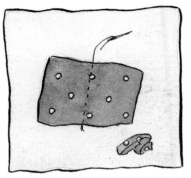

Step 4 Fold the tie in half so the pointed end forms the flap of the case. Pin edges together and sew using over and over stitch. It may not lie exactly flat as the middle section of the tie will be narrower than the wide end. Sew one half of the popper to the inside of the pointy flap. Check where the other half needs to go, and sew it on.

Step 5 If you'd like to add a bow, cut an 8-cm/3¼-in section from the middle of the tie. Take out the inner wadding. Hem, or leave the edge raw. (If you do hem, it's easier to press the edges in with an iron before sewing as little bits of silk can be very slippery.)

Step 6 Sew a gathering stitch up middle and pull tight to make a bow. Secure gathering with a few stitches on spot. Cover the middle with a thin oblong of tie – a perfect use for one of those little tidying strips mentioned in step 3. (These bows can be sewn on to anything – a hat, hairband, t-shirt, or plain metal barrettes to make a girlie hairslide.)

Make sure the tie is spotlessly clean. Even the merest trace of someone else's gravy will leave you feeling a bit queasy.

Button necklace •

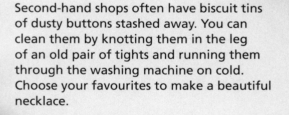

Second-hand shops often have biscuit tins of dusty buttons stashed away. You can clean them by knotting them in the leg of an old pair of tights and running them through the washing machine on cold. Choose your favourites to make a beautiful necklace.

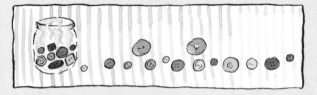

Step 1 It's a good idea to arrange your buttons on a table in roughly the order you want them to go – small at the outer edges and big in the middle, or by colour.

Step 2 Thread the needle with ribbon. Starting at one end of your design, thread the first button on to the needle, sliding it down the ribbon to about 25cm/10in from the end. Now put the next button upside down and thread it on the needle. Slide it down until it butts up against, and half covers, the first button. By turning every other button upside down your necklace looks good on both sides. Continue in this way until the necklace is the right length.

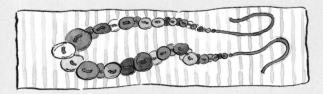

Step 3 Take off the needle and adjust the ribbons to the right length. Tie a knot at either end next to last buttons to stop them sliding off.

Silk-covered necklace and bangles

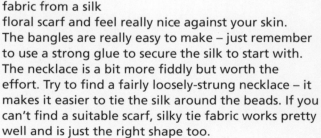

You will need
- Bangles
- Necklace
- Thin fabric – an old silk scarf or tie is ideal

Tools
- Scissors
- Pins
- Thread
- Fabric glue

These bangles and necklaces are wrapped in strips of fabric from a silk floral scarf and feel really nice against your skin. The bangles are really easy to make – just remember to use a strong glue to secure the silk to start with. The necklace is a bit more fiddly but worth the effort. Try to find a fairly loosely-strung necklace – it makes it easier to tie the silk around the beads. If you can't find a suitable scarf, silky tie fabric works pretty well and is just the right shape too.

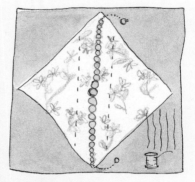  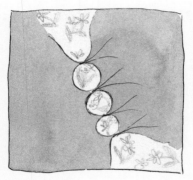

NECKLACE Step 1 Cut a long strip of silk about 2cm/¾in wider than the circumference of the widest bead and at least 20cm/8in longer than necklace. Cut on the bias if you can, it will make the fabric more pliable. On a square scarf that means from point to point, rather than along one edge. Ties are often already cut on the bias. You may need to join 2 strips together. Cut several lengths of thread about 20cm/8in long.

Step 2 Lie the beads on top of the silk. Dab glue on top of the central bead and stick the fabric to it. You shouldn't need to glue the other beads until you get to the last ones. When dry, bring the other side over, tucking the raw edge in. You may want to secure it temporarily with a pin.

Step 3 Now bind the fabric tightly on each side of the central bead, winding the thread several times round before knotting. Trim as close to the knot as you can. Now work out from the centre, wrapping, pinning, and binding each bead as you go. Turn the fabric edges under before securing the last beads – you may need to use glue for these.

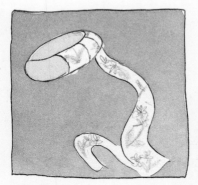

BANGLE Cut a long strip of silk about 12cm/5in wide. It's easier if on the bias, but not essential. Glue one end to the inside of the bangle and start winding around. As you wind, fold the raw edge over – this gives a neat finish. When you get back to the beginning, trim and tuck the end of fabric in and pin. Either secure it with a few small stitches or glue. You may need to use more than one strip.

Patches

See templates
pp.120-21 & 126-7

Jazz up your jeans, or anything else you want to make unique, with an appliqué patch. The best fabrics to use are those which don't fray, such as felt or t-shirt fabric. Other fabrics can either be turned in at the edges, or left with a raw edge which then becomes part of the look of the patch. Use any of the templates or create your own designs – it's a very simple way to create something unique. Cut out the templates, draw round on to the fabric and cut out. To make the fabric stiffer iron on some interfacing. This helps prevent fraying too. If you use Bondaweb, you can then stick the patch where you want it by simply ironing it on. Otherwise dab on a bit of fabric glue, or just pin and sew. The best stitches to use are over and over stitch, or running stitch.

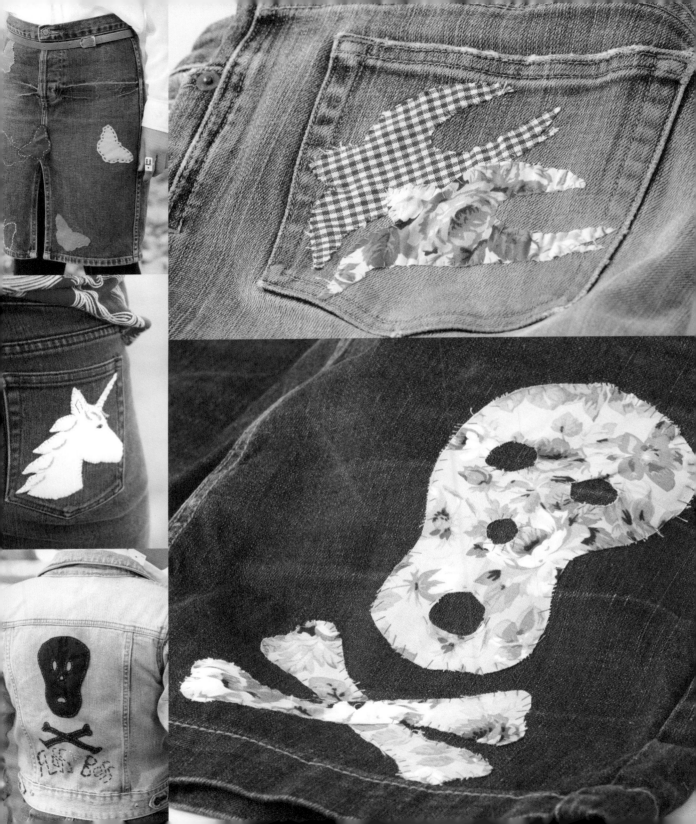

Bobble hat and fingerless gloves •

You will need

- Acrylic jumper – you could use a woollen material but it will fray a bit more and you might want to finish the cut edges with a blanket stitch
- For the gloves, fairly tight sleeves are ideal – say a smallish ladies size. You can make them from a larger jumper but you may need to take in a hefty hem along the side seam.
- Narrow ribbon, felt or fabric scraps, embroidery thread for decoration

Tools

- Sewing kit

These hat and gloves are so easy to make – there's hardly any sewing involved, so you'll have plenty of time to customize them. Try embroidery, appliqué, lace, ribbon or lacing.

HAT Step 1 The hat is made from a rectangle. Turn the jumper inside out. Measure your head. Halve the measurement, add on a 2-cm/¾-in seam allowance, and mark this out along the bottom edge of the jumper, starting from the right-hand seam. So, if your head measures 58cm/22¾in, mark out 31cm/12in (29cm/11¼in + 2cm/¾in). Using this as the bottom edge mark out a rectangle 28cm/11in high.

Step 2 Cut out the rectangle, leaving the right-hand seam intact. Pin the left-hand side and sew a 2-cm/¾-in seam. Turn the right way round.

Step 3 Sew a gathering thread all the way round the hat 8cm/3¼in below the top edge but don't pull it tight just yet. Now carefully make a series of vertical cuts, about 1cm/½in apart, from the top edge to within 5mm/¼in of the gathering thead. Pull the gathering thread tight and secure it by sewing several stitches on the spot. Try it on – if it's too long you can turn up a small hem. Your hat is now ready to decorate!

Step 4 If you can find a thick needle (we used a size 14 Yarn Darner) you can sew a narrow ribbon, no wider than 3mm, directly on to your hat without making any holes first. Try a line of stitches about 1cm/½in long, about 2cm/¾in from the bottom edge.

GLOVES Step 1 These gloves can be as long as you want. The basic technique is the same. Turn your jumper inside out and measure the length from the cuff end of the sleeve – 32cm/12½in is a good starting point for a mid-arm glove.

Step 2 Cut the sleeves off. Measure 6cm/2½in along the side seam from the cuff end. Mark out a small scoop about 4cm/1½in long. This is where your thumb will go. Make it a bit higher and smaller for a child, and a little bigger for a man. Cut out and try on. Make it bigger if necessary. If you want the sleeve part of the glove to be tighter, sew a sloping seam from the thumb hole to the cut end.

Step 3 Turn the gloves the right way round and decorate. We went for a biker motif with a small skull & crossbones and heart appliqué. Cut out small felt shapes using the templates on p.121 and p.127 as a guide. Pin on and sew. Using a pencil, carefully mark out 'LOVE' and 'HATE' on the gloves, spacing out the letters so they sit above your four fingers. Embroider using running stitch.

Paper pattern
lampshade
p.106

Record bowls
and clock
p.97

Decoupage
table p.98

Covered
notebooks p.109

Cotton reel pin-cushions
and jam jar sewing kit p.100

Old map picture
p.98

Home

ReCrafting is a great way of transforming boring Ikea-style furniture into unique one-offs for your home. Decoupage – the art of covering things with paper – is really quick and effective. We covered loads of tables with different designs, cutting up old maps, dictionaries, music books and comics to create some really quirky pieces. Old lampshades are another great find – whip off the old fabric and cover with paper patterns for an ethereal glow.

Owl doorstop
p.102

Dachshund draught excluder
p.104

Secret compartment book p.108

Knitted t-shirt rug p.110

Button picture •

See templates pp.120-21

You will need

- Picture frame – you won't need the glass
- Fabric for the background – we used a stripey shirt
- Buttons – we used about 60 in our picture

Tools

- Sewing kit
- Tailor's chalk
- Glue

Simple shapes work best in this project. If you don't fancy hearts, enlarge the butterfly or bird template. You could embroider names and a date underneath a heart like this and give it to someone as a wedding or anniversary present.

Step 1 Cut a rectangle of material about 5cm/2in bigger than the frame. Trace a template for the design, cut out, and draw round very lightly with tailor's chalk or a dressmaker's pencil.

Step 2 Arrange your buttons within the drawn line. When you're happy with your design, secure each one with a tiny dab of glue, avoiding holes.

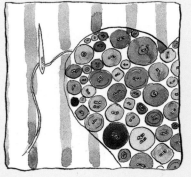

Step 3 When dry, sew the buttons to the background fabric with a single piece of thread.

Step 4 Cut a rectangle from cardboard to match the back of the frame.

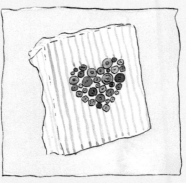

Step 5 Lay the picture button side down. Centre the cardboard on top. Glue the edges of cardboard and fold the fabric over, pulling tight to ensure there are no wrinkles. Fix in the frame.

Silver spoon and fork hooks

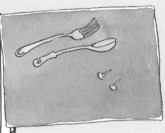

You will need
- Silver plated spoons and forks
- Chrome dome-headed screws

Tools
- Hammer (a rubber-tipped one is useful)
- Bradawl
- Electric drill
- Bolt – about 1.2cm/½in in diameter (for bending handles round)
- Vice – or similar

This is strangely satisfying. You don't need any special equipment – just basic DIY tools such as a hammer, a drill and bradawl. Flattening the spoons and forks is pretty easy – a few whacks and they start to go. The only thing where real strength is required is bending the handles up – we were feeling a bit wimpy after a hard day's crafting but Murray, Sarah's dad, bent them all in a few minutes.

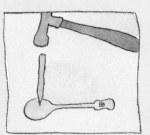

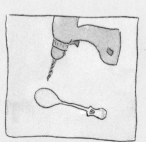

Step 1 Hold a spoon bowl side up on a block of wood and start tapping with the hammer. After a few blows it will start to flatten. Work your way out and round until the spoon is completely flat, turning it over as necessary.

Step 2 Use a bradawl to tap guide marks for the drill holes.

Step 3 Using a metal drill bit, drill holes. Use a hammer to tap down any rough edges from drilling.

Step 4 Mount the bolt securely in the vice. Place the handle over it and tap down with a rubber-tipped hammer till it bends.

Record bowl

Melting down your partner's, sister's or dad's precious vinyl into a set of snack bowls may trigger family friction. But just as there are some books you would never cut up, and others you are happy to see recycled, so too with records. James's collection of Sisters of Mercy 12 inches is safe – but the vast majority of charity shops shelter stacks and stacks of old LPs and singles unlikely ever to see a turntable again. The trick is to keep watching your records – it only takes a few seconds before they get pliable. Have oven gloves ready to whip the tray out as soon as they start getting floppy. I let one get too hot and it melted through the bars of the rack. Also think about the shape of your final bowl – after much experimenting we found a traditional mixing bowl gave the best shape.

You will need
- Old records

Tools
- Oven
- Assorted bowls – pudding basins, traditional mixing bowls
- Oven gloves

Step 1 Heat the oven to its highest temperature. On a tray – which doesn't need to be hot – invert a bowl. Centre the record over the bowl. Put in the oven – you don't need to close the door.

Step 2 Don't stop looking at the record. After about 30 seconds (this will vary depending on your oven) it will start to droop. Give it another 10 seconds and take the tray out. With oven gloves, shape the hot plastic around the bowl. You can also put another bowl on top and mould the plastic between the two.

Step 3 As the record cools, it will quickly become rigid again. You can heat and reshape it if it's not to your liking. If you want to put small things in it cover the central hole with two small circles of sticky tape.

Record clock

Turn an old record into a clock in a matter of seconds. See the one we made on p.92. You can buy the clock components from craft shops for a few pounds. Teenagers love these relics from the past – even if they've never seen a record player in their lives!

Decoupage tables •

You will need
- Table
- Sandpaper
- Paper
- PVA glue
- Varnish

Tools
- Scissors
- Paintbrush

This is an incredibly easy way to turn pieces of unloved old furniture into beautiful, quirky objects. It's quick and highly satisfying. You can use all kinds of printed material: old comics, maps, music scores, cookery books and dictionaries are easy to find in second-hand shops. Look for tables that don't have too many fiddly bits. It doesn't matter if they aren't very lovely to start with – they soon will be.

Although you can buy special decoupage glue, we found a well-watered PVA works just fine. With some older furniture, the varnish can seep through the covering paper. If this happens, let it dry, cover with one layer of oil-based varnish to seal it and continue. This didn't seem to be a problem with Ikea-era furniture. However its best to use a water-based varnish to finish your work as it doesn't discolour the paper so much.

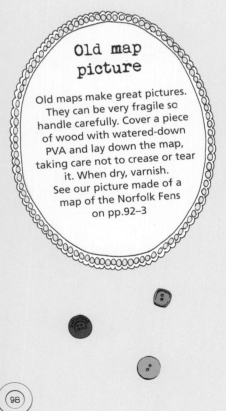

Old map picture

Old maps make great pictures. They can be very fragile so handle carefully. Cover a piece of wood with watered-down PVA and lay down the map, taking care not to crease or tear it. When dry, varnish. See our picture made of a map of the Norfolk Fens on pp.92–3

Step 1 Prepare your table. Lightly sand all the surfaces to be covered. You don't need to remove the original varnish or paint – you just want to roughen the surface. Prepare your printed material. We left some of the pages from a 1950s dictionary whole, but we cut up the Beano annual into cartoon squares. We cut the music into sections too.

Step 2 Water down the PVA. We found a 4-parts water to 1-part glue solution worked well.

Step 3 If you are going to paper the legs, turn the table upside down and start here. Work your way round the legs making sure none of the wood is showing through.

Step 4 Turn the table the right way up and cover the top. Leave to dry.

Step 5 When it is totally dry, seal with 4 or 5 coats of varnish, leaving each coat to dry completely in between.

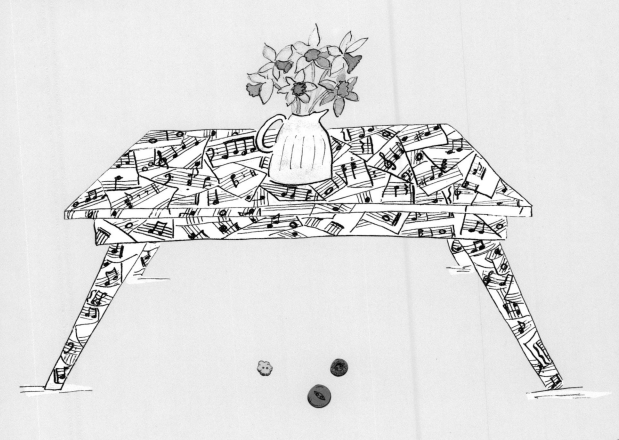

Cotton reel pin-cushions and jam jar sewing kit

As soon as you start sewing you will realize how much you need a pin-cushion. Otherwise your sofa will become a pin repository and you will be forever (guiltily) pulling pins from the soft soles of your children's feet. The jam jar sewing kit is a great way of keeping sewing essentials to hand – especially small things such as sewing threads or buttons.

COTTON REEL PIN-CUSHION Cut a circle of cardboard the same diameter as the top of the cotton reel. Cut a circle of fabric with a diameter 2cm/¾in bigger than the card. Sew a gathering stitch all the way round the edge of the fabric. Put a pinch of stuffing in the middle of the fabric. Put the cardboard circle inside and start pulling the thread until it is gathered tightly. You may want to adjust the amount of stuffing at this point. Secure the gathering with a few stitches. Use fabric glue to stick it to the top of the reel.

JAM JAR SEWING KIT Cut a fabric circle with a diameter 4cm/1½in bigger than the lid of your jam jar. Sew a gathering stitch all the way round. Glue a small handful of stuffing to the lid. Apply a thin line of glue to the edge of the lid. Place the fabric circle on top of stuffing and pull the thread tight. Stick the fabric down to the edge of the lid – an elastic band will help hold it in place while the glue is drying. When dry, trim any excess fabric and cover with a ribbon.

You will need
- Cotton reels
- Small pieces of fabric
- Jam jar
- Soft rags or toy stuffing
- Ribbon
- Elastic band

Tools
- Sewing kit
- Fabric glue

Owl doorstop

See templates p.121

You will need
- Tweed jacket – just the sleeves (or about half a metre/20 inches of fabric)
- Buttons
- Felt scrap
- Rice or sand

Tools
- Sewing kit
- Sewing machine

Owls are having a moment. They are everywhere; on plates, wallpaper, clothes, cushions. Pottery owls perch on shelves, cuddly owls nest on pillows. They are definitely the most fashionable bird around. The Owl House family has been one of the most popular sewing kits Buttonbag has ever done. Despite the predatory reality of the night hunter, fabric owls are just so... cute. This doorstop started life as the sleeves of a rather nice tweed jacket. You could use any other thick fabric – corduroy, velvet, even an old blanket. Filled with rice or sand the owl makes a very effective doorstop. Just don't be surprised if someone sneaks it off for a cuddle.

Step 1 Carefully unpick the sleeves and open out into 2 flat pieces. Cut off the cuffs in a straight line 2cm/¾in above the last buttonhole (which may well be fake buttonholes).

Step 2 Fold the first sleeve in half lengthways, right sides together. Draw a line up the outer edge and mark a point 40cm/16in up. Then measure and mark 35cm/15in up the centre fold. Join the 2 points with a shallow curve. Cut out and then cut an identical shape from the other sleeve.

Step 3 Using the template, cut a heart-shaped face from felt or other scrap fabric. Sew on buttons for eyes and a triangular beak. Sew to the right side of one owl body about 12cm/5in from the top (the shallow curve).

Step 4 Pin the owl bodies right sides together and machine sew both sides and the bottom. To make the owl stand up you need to create a gusset along the bottom seam. Squash each corner down matching bottom seam against side seam – it should look like a triangle. Pin in place. Draw a straight line across, about 5cm/2in from the point of the triangle. Sew.

Step 5 Turn the owl inside out and fill with rice or sand. Fold the top edges in and pin together. Sew closed with stitches small enough to prevent any rice from spilling out.

Step 6 For the wings, undo the button and buttonhole pieces of the cuffs. If they are fake (most jackets are) you will need to cut off the buttons. Shorten each buttonhole piece to about 10cm/4in. Hem and hand sew to the body.

Baby owl bookend

Scale down the owl and you will have a baby owl bookend. It could also be a paperweight but, in the age of email, these have gone out of fashion. However, you might still find an aged relative with a penchant for stacking bills neatly who might appreciate one.

Dachshund draught excluder

See templates pp.124-5

You will need
- A pair of trousers – the longer the better if you're making a draught excluder
- Felt scraps for ears
- Stuffing or finely cut-up soft rags or socks
- Rice – this makes the legs nice and heavy
- Buttons

Tools
- Sewing kit
- Sewing machine

Even if you don't have any draughts you might want to make a sausage dog. Isaac was so smitten by this dachshund, he insisted on cutting up his favourite cords to make one for himself. It was the first time he'd used a sewing machine and he managed really well. Floppy, the sausage dog, is now in permanent residence on his pillow.

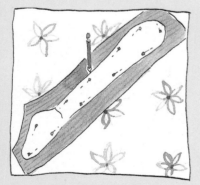

Step 1 Using the template, turn the trousers inside out and pin the face to the top of the leg (you might need to unpick a back pocket so you can use the full length). Extend the body all the way down the leg creating a rounded rump at the hem end. Cut through both thicknesses to give 2 body shapes.

Step 2 Trace and cut out tail, leg and ear patterns and cut 8 legs, 2 tails and 2 ears from other trouser leg or from felt scraps.

Step 3 Pin each pair of legs wrong sides together and sew round leaving the top open. Fill two-thirds full with rice. Sew across the top. Pin the tails wrong sides together. Stitch the long sides together and stuff with rags or wadding.

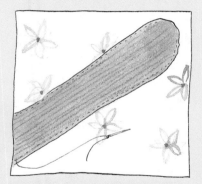

Step 4 Pin the body shapes right sides together and machine or hand sew all the way round leaving a 12-cm/5-in gap for stuffing at the tail end. Notch the seam, turn the right way round and stuff.

Step 5 Pin the tail into gap left for stuffing, sew it into place and close the gap. Pin on legs and hand sew.

Step 6 Hand sew ears into place and sew on buttons for eyes.

Paper pattern lampshade

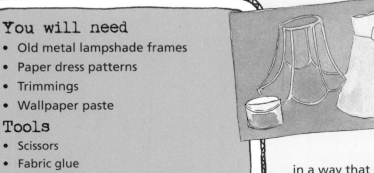

You will need
- Old metal lampshade frames
- Paper dress patterns
- Trimmings
- Wallpaper paste

Tools
- Scissors
- Fabric glue
- Small paint brush

Old paper dress patterns are made from a very fine tissue paper and work really well as a covering for metal framed lampshades. As the tissue dries it contracts and tightens in a way that helps define the shape. We also like the way you see two patterns – one from the overlapping tissue and one from the printed cutting lines and instructions.

Step 1 Cut the paper patterns into strips long enough to reach across two bars in the lampshade and between 4cm/1½in and 8cm/3¼in wide.

Step 2 Mix up a fairly liquid wallpaper paste mix. Cover the first paper strip entirely with paste (a plastic mat or table cloth or lots of newspaper is useful here for the floor and work surface) and drape it over the first two bars of the lampshade, about 2cm/¾in below the top rim. Work your way round adding more strips, generously overlapping each one.

Step 3 Cover the entire lampshade with paper strips. When you get near the bottom, balance the lampshade on a bottle or bowl so you can take the last row of paper strips right over the bottom rim. When it is entirely dry, patch any small holes that you may have missed. Leave to dry again. Use scissors to trim excess paper from top and bottom. Stick on a trim with fabric glue.

Hot water bottle cover

You will need
- Chunky polo neck jumper – the thicker and softer the better
- Felt and fabric scraps for decorating
- Narrow ribbon
- Hot water bottle

Tools
- Sewing kit

On cold winter nights everybody needs a cosy hot water bottle to cuddle up to. A polo neck jumper makes a perfect cover, with the actual neck covering the top of the bottle. We used a cable knit jumper made out of a lovely soft lambswool.

A thicker jumper is ideal here so you can cuddle without getting burnt. Decorate and personalize with felt, fabric scraps and embroidery.

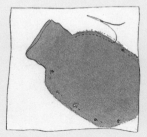

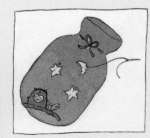

Step 1 Turn the jumper inside out and lay flat. The polo neck becomes the opening to the cover, so it has to be able to stretch enough to get the bottle in. Lay your hot water bottle on top, with the 'shoulders' of the bottle level with the bottom of the neck of the jumper, and draw round, about 1.5cm/½in outside the edge of the bottle. You can decorate your bottle now (see step 4) or do it as the final stage.

Step 2 Pin the 2 sides together, and cut out just outside the drawn line. Using embroidery or any strong thread, sew a running stitch all around. Turn the cover the right way round again.

Step 3 Thread the narrow ribbon on to your needle and, starting at the centre front, sew a gathering stitch around the polo neck at the level where the bottom of the neck of the bottle will come. When the bottle is inside you can then pull this ribbon tight and tie in a bow at the front.

Step 4 If you haven't yet done so, decorate with felt or fabric scraps, and embroidery.

Secret compartment book

Choose a big hardback book. Draw a rectangle on the page you are going to start cutting. Using a ruler and a sharp craft knife, carefully cut the rectangle out through all the pages. We sealed the cut edges by painting them with PVA glue. This makes a more box-like compartment within the book. Children love secret compartment books.

Covered • notebooks

Covering notebooks, albums or diaries with beautiful fabric is really effective and they make great presents. You can simply cut a rectangle larger than the outer cover and glue it on – we did this with a denim skirt, so you get a nifty pocket on the cover too. However our favourite foolproof way is to sew it. See p.127 for the pattern.

Knitted t-shirt rug

You will need
- 12 t-shirts

Tools
- Knitting needles
- Sewing kit

You can knit with almost anything. We cut up a pile of old t-shirts to make this rug. One large man's t-shirt knits up into a square of approximately 25cm/10in. And it's a myth that you need really big needles – we used a pair of regular 5mm/USA size 8 bamboo needles for this rug. The trick is to try and keep your stitches as loose as possible. You can make this rug as big as you like by adding more strips. We used twelve t-shirts in four rows of three which makes a decent sized rug for the hearth, bedside or bathroom.

Step 1 Starting at the bottom hem, cut each t-shirt into a long thin strip, about 1.5cm/½in wide spiralling all the way up so you have one long piece. You don't need to measure it – cut by eye and if the thickness varies it won't be a big problem.

Step 2 Wind each cut-up t-shirt into a ball so you don't get in a mess.

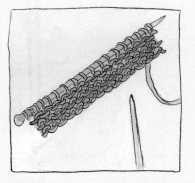

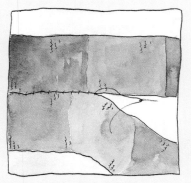

Step 3 Using 5mm/USA size 8 needles – or a little bigger if that's what you have – cast on 17 stitches or thereabouts and knit away. If you want a very regular geometric pattern, count the number of rows knitted and repeat the same number for each t-shirt. Start knitting with the smallest and you won't run out.

Step 4 When you are nearly at the end of the first t–shirt, knot the end to the next t-shirt strip and carry on. Knit the first 3 t-shirts together and count your rows. Cast off. Make 3 more strips in the same way ensuring each strip is made up of the same number of rows.

Step 5 Use embroidery thread or another strong thread to join all 4 strips together. Push any knots where you joined 2 strips together through to the other side.

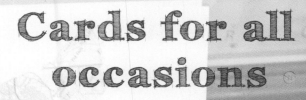

Cards for all occasions

Simple shapes cut from scraps of books, comics and fabric make great greetings cards. We used various templates to create these. Our favourites include valentine hearts carved from the pages of Mills & Boons novels, Christmas trees and baubles from an old book of carols, musical swallows and baby booties from scraps of jumpers.

I WANT CAKE AND I WANT IT NOW

Christmas decorations •

See templates pp.124-5

You will need

- Fabric scraps
- Buttons
- Ribbon
- Stuffing or finely cut-up soft rags or old socks

Tools

- Sewing kit

Unpacking the Christmas decorations our children have made or we made when we were kids is one of our favourite bits about Christmas. You can make little tree decorations out of pretty much any fabric you can find. We made these from small scraps of jumpers left over from other projects in the book and even tinier pieces of Liberty print. They are very easy to hand sew and they look really sweet hanging in little groups – they don't take very long either!

Step 1 Trace template and cut out. Pin the shape to double thickness of fabric and cut out.

Step 2 Pin the shapes together and hand sew all the way round the edge using a simple over and over stitch. When you have nearly reached the end push a little stuffing in and sew closed.

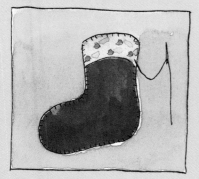

Step 3 For the robins, stockings and bells: cut out robin breasts and stocking and bell trim from a contrasting fabric. Pin into place and sew. Push a pinch of stuffing in before you reach the end and sew closed.

Step 4 Sew buttons on to the front of your tree and bauble shapes. Add a ribbon loop at the top of each decoration for hanging.

Templates

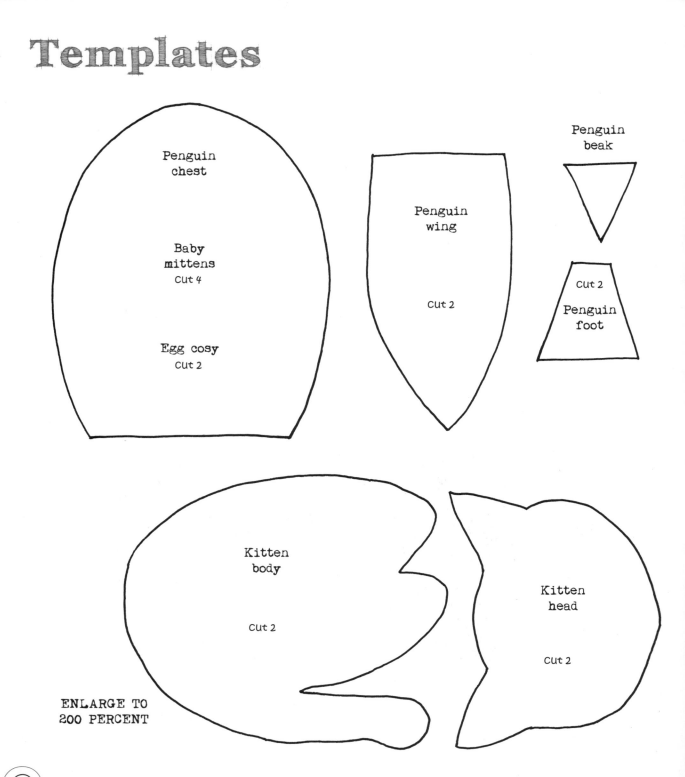

Penguin
beak

Penguin
chest

Baby
mittens
Cut 4

Egg cosy
Cut 2

Penguin
wing

Cut 2

Cut 2

Penguin
foot

Kitten
body

Cut 2

Kitten
head

Cut 2

ENLARGE TO
200 PERCENT

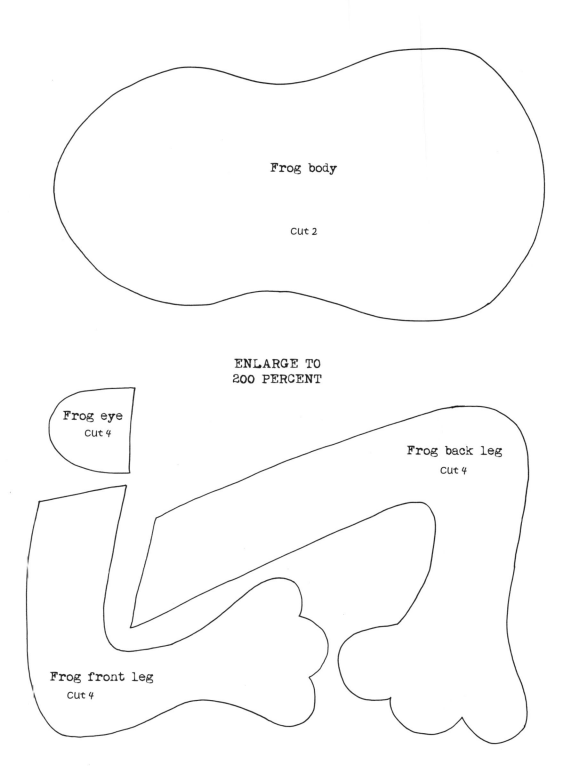

Frog body

Cut 2

ENLARGE TO
200 PERCENT

Frog eye
Cut 4

Frog back leg
Cut 4

Frog front leg
Cut 4

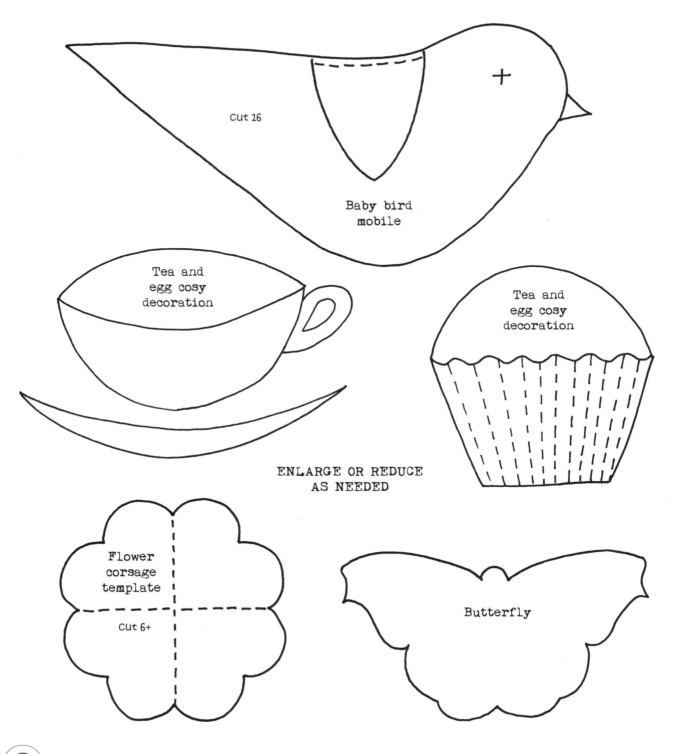

Cut 16

Baby bird
mobile

Tea and
egg cosy
decoration

Tea and
egg cosy
decoration

ENLARGE OR REDUCE
AS NEEDED

Flower
corsage
template

Cut 6+

Butterfly

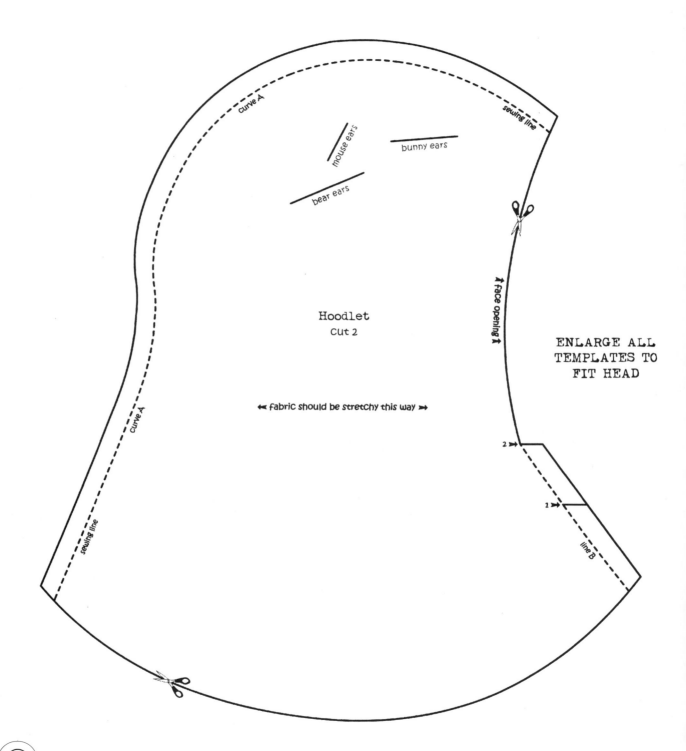

curve A

sewing line

mouse ears

bunny ears

bear ears

Hoodlet
Cut 2

↕ face opening ↕

ENLARGE ALL
TEMPLATES TO
FIT HEAD

curve A

◄◄ fabric should be stretchy this way ►►

sewing line

2 ►►

1 ►►

line B

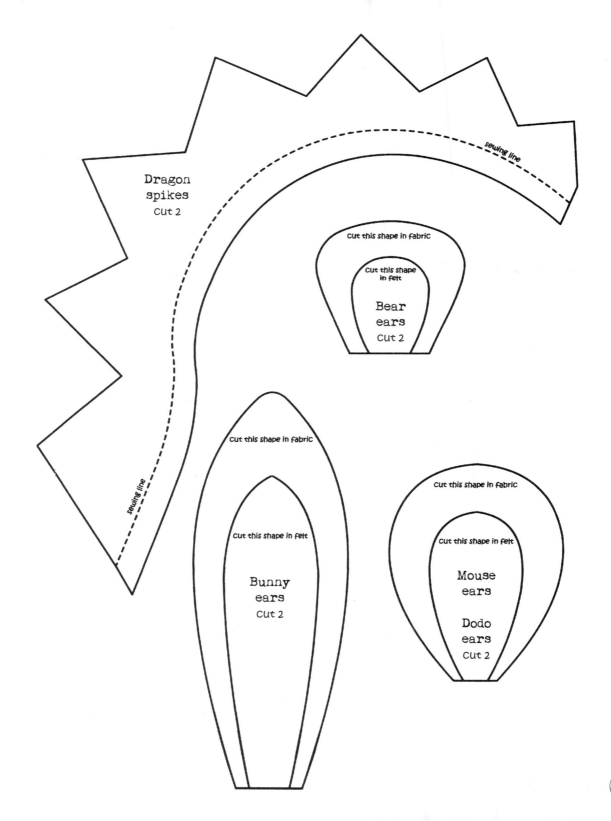

Dragon
spikes
Cut 2

sewing line

sewing line

Cut this shape in fabric

Cut this shape
in felt

Bear
ears
Cut 2

Cut this shape in fabric

Cut this shape in felt

Bunny
ears
Cut 2

Cut this shape in fabric

Cut this shape in felt

Mouse
ears

Dodo
ears
Cut 2

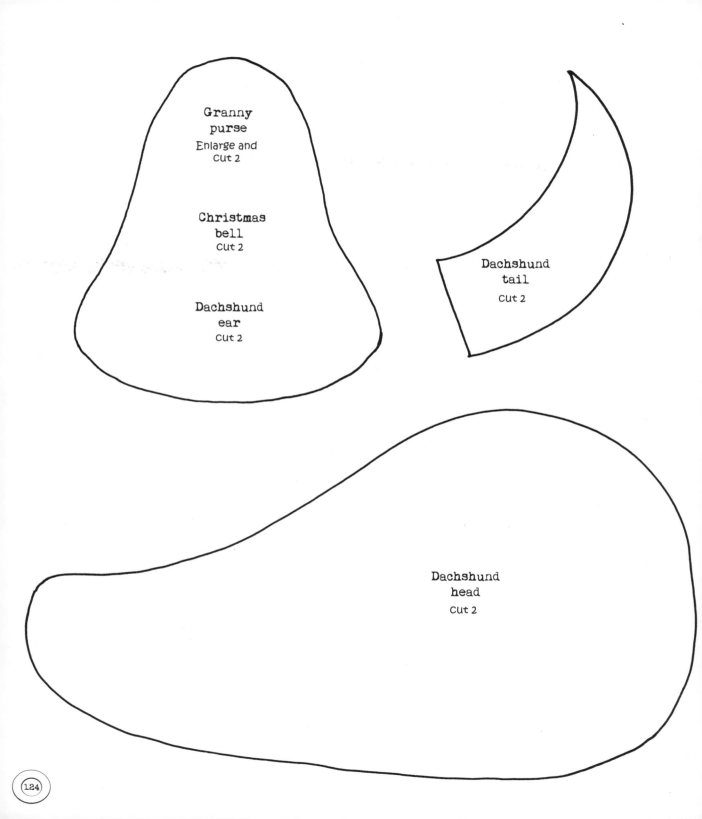

Granny
purse
Enlarge and
Cut 2

Christmas
bell
Cut 2

Dachshund
ear
Cut 2

Dachshund
tail
Cut 2

Dachshund
head
Cut 2

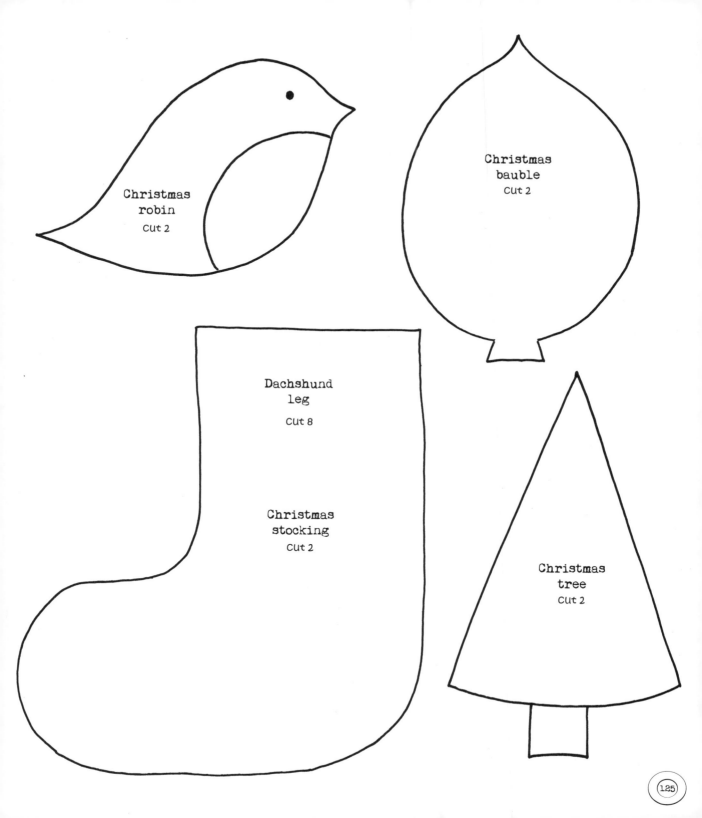

Christmas
robin
Cut 2

Christmas
bauble
Cut 2

Dachshund
leg
Cut 8

Christmas
stocking
Cut 2

Christmas
tree
Cut 2

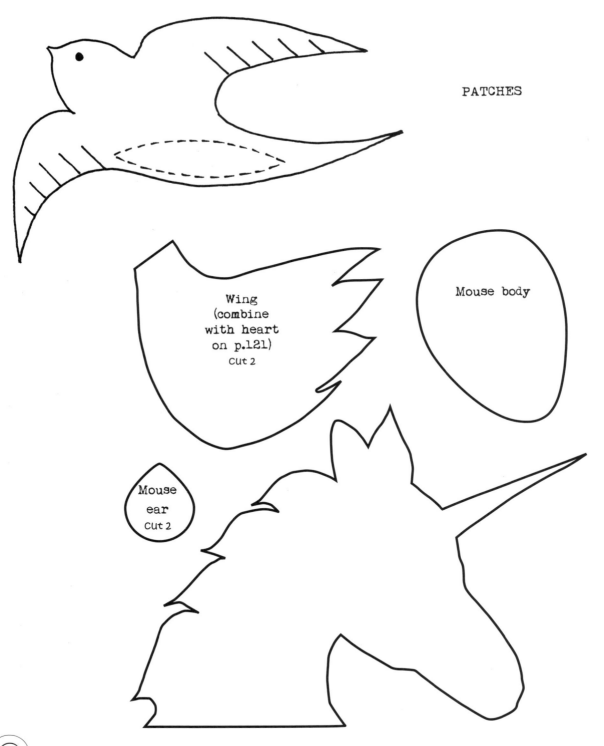

PATCHES

Wing
(combine
with heart
on p.121)
Cut 2

Mouse body

Mouse
ear
Cut 2

COVERED NOTEBOOKS

Cut a rectangle of fabric 4cm/1½in higher than the book to be covered and twice the width, plus spine, plus the width of the book again x 2 plus 2cm (to create a pocket for each cover). Pattern facing up, fold and pin a 10-cm/4-in hem along both the short edges, folding the last 1cm/½in back on itself. Now sew the fabric lengthways 2cm/¾in from the top and 2cm/¾in from the bottom. Turn the right way round and carefully slip front and back covers into the pockets.

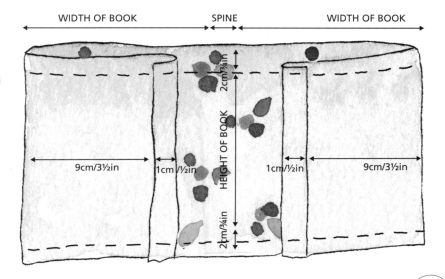

WIDTH OF BOOK   SPINE   WIDTH OF BOOK

9cm/3½in   1cm/½in   2cm/¾in   HEIGHT OF BOOK   2cm/¾in   1cm/½in   9cm/3½in   2cm/¾in